The Flight of the Cuckoo

J. Alan Brown

By the author of Out of Sight Out of Mind.

**In the neighbouring Warwickshire mining villages,
natives of Dordon were known as "Cuckoos"
due to their alleged attempt to keep a
cuckoo in a field by closing the gate,
a feat usually ascribed to the
Wise Men of Gotham.**

© J. Alan Brown, 2019. All rights reserved.
Cover photograph: Getty Images

For Ellen, Sarah, Lugh and Finn
This is your story, too...

and in memory of my two great school friends,
Neville Ivor Ball and Eric Francis James Turney,
both taken long before their time.

Contents

Preface

1. A Tale of two grandfathers
2. Not so silent movies
3. War in the village
4. Aren't you the boy. . .?
5. There's no business like show business
6. First Innings
7. The learning curve
8. More play, less work
9. Final fling
10. Grounded
11. To Cincinnati and beyond
12. The little hut on the canal bank
13. North to Scotland
14. Life beyond the wall
15. Oil on troubled waters
16. Scotsport
17. One false move
18. Uncharted territory
19. Going Dutch

Postscript

Preface

One thing you cannot do with family history is begin at the beginning, so I can only start from the point at which it becomes coherent. After all, it is of little consequence to me to know that I am the great-great-great grandson of John Callendar and Margaret Burnett if the only other thing I know about them is that they lived in 18th century Scotland.

I now regret that I did not listen more carefully when my father talked of his childhood during the Great War and that I did not ask so many of the questions he is no longer around to answer. I know that he felt the same about his lack of knowledge of his own father's early life, much of which was spent in India.

As a result, only brief glimpses can be seen of lives which must have been so different to our own.

I cannot vouch that all the stories that follow are entirely true, since they are subject to the uncertainty of memory, but all characters are real, although in some instances I have changed their names to avoid embarrassment.

To anyone I may have treated unfairly, I apologise.

Being the youngest son of a youngest son extends the time and changes over a mere three generations, but with the increasing pace of life nowadays, my own grandsons may find the world I inhabited for the first forty years of my life covered here were just as strange as I find that of my grandparents.

I hope they will want to find out.

A Tale of Two Grandfathers

It came as quite a surprise to me to learn only recently that my "Irish" and "Scottish" grandfathers were both born within a few miles of each other in London and within a year of each other in 1866 and 1867.

Though my personal knowledge of them was limited to the first eight years of my life, they both made a strong impression on me in very different ways.

To my young eyes, my paternal grandfather, Walsingham Brown, was a large, stern and rather frightening old man who, even in his eighties, still dominated those of his family who still lived under his roof.

I learned that he had run away from home in his youth and together with his brother had joined the 5th Royal Irish Lancers, serving most of his enlistment in India. He told tales of "suttee", the outlawed but still practised ritual suicide of widows on the funeral pyres of their husbands and of the soldiers raking through the ashes to find unmelted coins, which, however well polished, the local traders would recognise and refuse to accept.

After his return to England in 1897, Walsingham, or 'Wals', as he was known, joined the prison service, first at Derby then at Nottingham, until his retirement in 1927. He also volunteered for the grisly duty of sitting with condemned prisoners as they awaited execution.

Evidence of the compassion of this rather stern character can be found in a letter, now in my possession. Written by the son of a convicted murderer, it thanks my grandfather for the kindness shown during the condemned man's final days.

Not, perhaps, the reaction to be expected from the family of an executed man to his gaoler.

A man from whom the occasional emotional outburst was not unknown, Wals once rushed into the house, having been summoned to the prison in an emergency. He loudly demanded a cup of tea as he hurriedly donned his uniform. As his unfortunate family was unable to produce the required beverage with sufficient speed, he cursed them roundly, removed the flowers from a vase, drank the foul contents, replaced the blooms and ran from the house.

On one occasion during a friendly game of cards, a friend of my father was ordered from the house for saying, "You don't seem to be having much luck, Mr. Brown!"

I am told I am a bit like old Wals!

Whilst he was clearly an irascible and serious minded individual, it would be unfair not to give an example of his bizarre sense of humour.

On his return from work one day, he announced to the children that he had just seen a water otter in a nearby stream. When the children arrived at the spot, however, there was no sign of life. Their interest was rekindled when their father reported a second sighting in the same place. He took them to the stream and pointed to an old, rusting kettle lying in the mud.
"That's not a water otter," the children complained.
"Well, what do you think it's for?" he replied.

One of his more serious claims was that he had traced his family tree back to the Elizabethan spy-master, Sir Francis Walsingham. Just where, apart from his Christian name, he got that little titbit from is unclear, since I have seen a letter he wrote in 1909 asking the Registry of Births, Deaths and Marriages for a copy of his birth certificate. He gave his details as Walsingham W. Brown, born 15th June 1867 at 10 Cambridge Square, Bethnal Green (now 197 Latimer Road).

The reply, conveniently scribbled on the original letter, indicated that searches of the registers of neighbouring Kensington and Fulham showed no trace of his birth!

While he was performing his deeds of derring-do in India, his future wife, Agnes Watts, was in domestic service as a laundry maid at Middlethon Hall, Long Parish, in Berkshire until 1893 when she attained a more advanced position at Castle Ashby in Northants, where her sister was already in charge of the laundry. How she came to meet her future husband is not recorded.

My father, William, was the youngest of seven children, with three brothers and three sisters. One brother, Harry, died in his youth of what was then called consumption, which probably explains my father's extreme concern whenever I or my brother suffered from a cough.

Another of my dad's brothers, George, joined the Territorial Army, mainly to have a smart uniform for Sundays, but was of course called up when World War One broke out and served with the Royal Field Artillery in France. Having seen most of his mates killed or wounded in the first two years of the war, he finally fell towards the end of the battle of the Somme and is buried in the military corner of the civilian cemetery at St. Pol.

On the night he died, George's distinctive whistle woke the family, who thought he had arrived home on leave. Official confirmation took longer to arrive.

The other brother, Walter, had emigrated to New Zealand aboard the emigrant ship "Somerset" eighteen months before the war started and returned with the Anzacs, only to be wounded at Gallipoli. After the war he returned to his adopted homeland and later became chief of the Fire Brigade in Wanganui.

My father's three sisters, Nell, Daisy and May, all lived to a ripe old age, with Daisy eventually supplementing the growing New Zealand branch of the family.

Like my paternal grandfather, my mother's father, David Hutchison, also lost contact with his family, in this instance because he married a girl considered 'unsuitable'. Although he was born in Mile End in the East End of London, he had obviously originated from a fairly well-to-do family, as photos of him as a baby in the mid-1860s shows him in the arms of the maid. He was later sent away to be educated at Loughborough School.

His father, also David, was born in Culross in Fife and following his initial education at the Culross Parish School spent five years there from 1849 to 1853 as an apprenticed student teacher, before gaining a Queen's Scholarship and moving to Glasgow Normal School.

After final qualification, he left Scotland and, married to another teacher, Annie Herriot Agnew, set up home in Mile End, where their daughter and three sons were born.

Sometime after the death of their daughter in 1869, the family moved to School House at Nailstone in Leicestershire. There, David junior, a keen practitioner of the new pastime of photography, succeeded in taking a picture of the ghostly lady who often appeared on the staircase.

The teenage David's mother died in Nailstone and he recalled riding on horseback to bring the doctor when she was stricken with her fatal illness.

What happened to his two brothers is unknown, although one, Thomas, is thought to have emigrated to America.

Though I only remember him in his eighties, my grandfather was apparently an athletic young man who once walked from Nottingham to Loughborough to play in an Old Boys cricket match, before walking back again afterwards.

He was set to follow his father's profession until his insistence in marrying a girl of whom his father disapproved caused him to be cut off penniless. His decision seems to have been justified, however, by over half a century of marriage to Louisa Franklin.

The couple met through the medium, if you will pardon the pun, of the Spiritualist Church, she as a faith healer and he as a young man who attended a meeting as a lark but stayed to become a convert. His conversion may have been hastened by the strange experience of being received by the minister expressing his gratitude that he had decided to attend on that evening as their regular organist was unwell! How the minister knew that David was a skilled performer on the organ, he never found out.

It may be imagined, however, that a Spiritualist healer would have a hard time convincing a dour and respectable Scot of her suitability as a daughter in law!

Their marriage produced a son who died in infancy and four daughters, the youngest of which became my mother.

The daughters were continually making and breaking alliances, vying for parental affection and finally splitting into two camps that effectively tore the family apart. This must have greatly saddened the dear old man that I remember as the embodiment of kindness.

By the time I was old enough to remember him he was very frail and almost totally deaf, but whenever I arrived to visit him, he would take a key from his waistcoat pocket and hand it to me. I would then unlock the sideboard drawer and always find a little gift. No surprise visit ever caught him unprepared or the drawer empty.

I used to love to visit his three-storeyed house on Alberta Terrace in Nottingham. For someone who had always lived in a bungalow, a house with two sets of stairs was wonderful. Like many old houses in Nottingham, it also had a cellar, a sinister and eerie place, where milk and coal coexisted peacefully. Whitewashed at its entrance, in the area where dairy products were stored, it wound down beyond the coal chute and disappeared into the blackness of the underworld.

After his father disowned him, my grandfather worked for the Post Office, ending his career in charge of the sorting office at Nottingham Central. This gave him an extensive knowledge of the location of almost every village and hamlet in Britain.

My parents and I were visiting when he

died. Some family reminiscences had sent him to bed laughing the night before, but he did not get up the following morning. He lay semi-conscious during the morning and died peacefully in the afternoon.

He had been my last surviving grandparent. I remember nothing of either of my grandmothers and it struck me as rather sad that all my grandparents had passed on by the time I was eight years old.

Not-so-silent movies

After the return to New Zealand of the wounded Walter and the death on the Somme of George, Grandad Brown was transferred from Derby to Nottingham prison, a simple commute nowadays but requiring relocation in those times.

So by 1917 my father's family had moved to Nottingham, where my father finished his school career by making ration books and then started his adult life and his passion for motorcycles.

It was no disadvantage that he lived on the same street as the Brough Superior motorcycle factory, for while he could never aspire to own one of the Rolls Royce of two wheeled transport, he was happy to test ride the new machines. Since he did so free of charge, no doubt George Brough was quite happy with the arrangement.

Team games, especially cricket, at which he had excelled sufficiently to represent the county at schoolboy level, would always remain dear to him, but after leaving school the long and unsociable hours of his work as a cinema projectionist meant that he would have little opportunity for these pastimes until well into his thirties.

This made motorcycling an ideal pastime for him, for it was something he could do in his own time. It was certainly more than just a means of transport to him, for he retained one long after the family car had been added to the list of chattels.

Amazing as it seems nowadays, my father claimed that the shortage of specialist garages obliged him to purchase his petrol from chemists' shops!

One of his favourite stories of his early motorcycling days concerns an occasion when he and some friends were searching for a suitable venue for a motorcycle trial. This is an event where competitors encounter observed sections of difficult terrain which they must negotiate without putting a foot onto the ground. Having found a rocky hillside my father and his friends spent a frustrating afternoon trying to find a way to climb it.

They had just decided that it was too difficult to include in the itinerary of their trial when an elderly farmer riding a motorcycle and sidecar arrived on the scene and ascended the hill without hesitation. He explained that he made the trip every day as it was a shortcut between two of his fields!

My father's other fascination was his work in the burgeoning industry of the cinema, at a time when the new 'electric theatres' were springing up across the country.

His job was at the Berridge Road Cinema, just around the corner from the house where lived a Post Office employee and his four feisty daughters.

In those far off days, movies were silent. This meant that musicians were employed to set the mood for the film and sheet music was delivered to the cinema along with the film itself. The smaller auditoria would have a pianist, but the Berridge boasted an orchestra of five musicians.

If 'orchestra' seems a grand title for a quintet, I recall that my Uncle Ernest, my Aunt May's husband, was leader of the Ernest Allen Dance Orchestra, which also consisted of five musicians. As a matter of fact, we must have been quite a musical lot in those days, since not only was Aunt Daisy's other half, Fred, a denizen of the orchestra pit at Nottingham Playhouse, but my father sometimes stood in as an extra clarinetist with Uncle Ernie's band on the rare occasions when his cinema duties permitted.

I know that Ernie's outfit won an annual 'Melody Maker' award in London, but have no idea how good the Berridge orchestra was since only one fact about them has been passed down to posterity.

They could play the National Anthem in under five seconds.

That is without the 'send him/her victorious' bit, of course, but nevertheless quite an achievement and it was a really fit audience who could exit the cinema quicker than the orchestra.

There were also sound effects in the silent movie era. For instance, copies of 'The Four Horsemen of the Apocalypse' arrived with a quantity of 'bombs', to be detonated at the climax of the film. On the last night of the film's run at the Berridge, my dad's assistant projectionist, Elmo, was despatched to the boiler room to wire up the bomb for the final performance. The boiler room had been chosen because of the pleasing, resonant 'boom' effect that it had produced during the week.

Elmo noticed that, whilst only one bomb was required, there were still five left. As it seemed a shame to waste them, he wired up all five.

At the climax of the film, the audience were rocked by the enormous blast from the boiler room. They thrilled to the clatter of flying debris. They were gripped with wonder by the fall of real plaster. Finally, they ran like hell when they thought the roof was going to collapse on them.

It didn't, of course, but famine, pestilence, disease and death was visited upon Elmo's pay packet for some considerable time thereafter.

As time went by, talkies came in and my father, now married and with the addition of the guy who would later become my big brother Dave, decided to acquire his own cinema, a decision which was to bring him to live and work in Dordon, a North Warwickshire village so obscure that even his father-in-law, the Postmaster, had never heard of it.

War in the village

The very first thing I remember is being dragged from my bed, wrapped in a blanket and hustled down the long corridor that ran through the centre of our bungalow. My mother's words of comfort were lost on me in my grizzling sleepiness.

Suddenly we were out of the house and surrounded by light brighter than day. Fire and phosphorus had bleached the colour from everything and lit the scene in a searing white. We then plunged back into darkness as we entered our Andersen shelter for the first and only time it was used in anger.

I remember the shelter best as a play house, equipped as it was with two bunk beds and a permanently muddy floor. What protection it would have offered if put to the test is hard to say, but my father used to say that it would at least save the authorities the trouble of burying us.

The bomb had landed between our bungalow and the farm house next door, leaving a crater which later developed into duck pond.

Elsewhere in the village houses were hit and a girl who would later be a classmate at school was lifted from the debris of her home, the only survivor. Her father, the only member of her family absent from home, took shelter a few streets away and was the only fatality when that house also took a hit.

Outside the village, a bomb with acres of pasture on which to fall harmlessly, picked out and obliterated an isolated farm cottage.

The war was not a regular visitor to our village, which merely had the misfortune to stand in the flight path between Germany and the industrial Midlands.

Like most families, mine had become used to the nightly routine of hearing first the sirens, then the incoming bombers and finally, after the homeward survivors had passed overhead, the 'All Clear'. As a result, the novelty of taking to the shelters soon gave way to late night darts matches. That is why, on the one night the bombers did not just pass over, despite the air raid warning, the surprise was total.

My father, who was in charge of the local Air Raid Precautions, was on patrol that night along with two wardens, one of whom was a lady.

They stood and gazed in amazement at the sight of a Heinkel bomber streaking up the main street of the village at little more than rooftop height, under fire from a night fighter. So engrossed were they in the spectacle that they forgot that real bullets were being fired, until one struck a kerbstone and sent a shower of debris in their direction.

The two gallant gentlemen dived to the ground and the lady was struck a glancing blow on the head by a small piece of pavement. The wound was minor but like many superficial head wounds, it bled profusely, causing the good lady to faint.

Her colleague, trying to render her assistance, loosened her collar and then promptly dropped his illicit cigarette down the front of her blouse. This was an eventuality not covered in the ARP handbook and despite the shortage of tobacco the hapless warden felt that any attempt at retrieval would breach the boundaries of good comradeship. He was becoming reconciled to his loss when the unmistakeable smell of burning convinced him that the second injury could become more serious than the first and that action would have to be taken. Eventually the poor victim of friendly fire and collateral damage recovered more embarrassed than injured.

The Heinkel was finally downed on a farm outside the next village where, it was whispered, the crew were greeted pointedly by a group of pitchfork-wielding Land Army girls.

Apart from this special night, our village, centred on coal mines and surrounded by farm land, was a contributor to the war rather than a participant in it. Khaki, Navy and Air Force blue were not too common a sight, compared to blackened faces and miners' helmets.

We did get occasional glimpses of the outside world, however. Our bungalow stood on a hill, with meadows to the rear which ran down to the river. One day, I remember that my brother Dave had taken me down to the pasture by the river to hear the horses farting, when an even greater sound rent the air. We were then engulfed by the shadow of a Wellington bomber as it skimmed above us. My brother identified the waving pilot as the Polish officer who lodged at the neighbouring farm. After this introduction, it became his custom to treat us to an exhibition of low level flying whenever he was in the area. It was amazing to stand on top of the hill and actually be able to look down on this huge aircraft as it flew along the river.

We also had a passing acquaintance with our allies, the Americans, whose long convoys of trucks would thread along Watling Street, the ancient Roman road which cut a tangent across the northern edge of the village.

Their trucks were the biggest vehicles we had ever seen and we kids would rush to watch them pass, in the hope of them throwing gum, or perhaps even catching a rare glimpse of a black man.

We also saw the enemy - Italian prisoners from the POW camp a few miles down the road. Their uniforms had large yellow patches sewn on the back, to identify them as prisoners and give their guards something to aim at if they tried to escape.

Many gave their parole and were allowed out to work on the local farms and for some of them it was the best life they had ever known. Indeed, some stayed on after the war, married into local farmers' families and started new lives far from their native soil.

Occasionally, some of the prisoners would be marched from the camp under guard to go to my father's cinema. They would sit in a row by themselves and if they made it past the newsreel, all would be well. All too often, however, the news would contain footage ridiculing Mussolini or detailing the latest Italian retreat and, to the jeers of the rest of the audience, the 'Eyeties' would file out silently and return to camp, often leaving their guards to enjoy the film.

On one memorable occasion, we even saw our exotic Russian allies, even though we had to go to nearby Tamworth to do so. Without a trace of snow on their boots, a group of Cossack horsemen did their bit for the allied cause by giving a demonstration of tent pegging and other equestrian military skills.

Hardly relevant in the context of the tank battles being slugged out on the steppes, perhaps, but a nice thought anyway.

Impressed as I was by the skills of the horsemen, I must confess I was more interested in the Harvard trainer plane whose American pilot had crashed into the river which ran by the showground.

Although my father nominally ran the village cinema, during the war most of the running was done by my mother, since dad worked by day for the Air Ministry in Coventry and patrolled the village by night as Head Warden of the ARP.

All cinemas had been closed at the outbreak of war, but, unlike the fledgling television service which was halted for the duration, they were soon reopened when their propaganda value had been recognised. So much so that when the maximum age for aircrew was increased and my father volunteered he was turned down not because of his Air Ministry or ARP duties but because it was thought more important to ensure the cinema stayed open.

One feature of the war which hit our village as hard as anywhere else was rationing. Wartime shortages meant that a variety of foods and household necessities could not be obtained by money alone, but only when accompanied by the necessary government issued coupons, which were intended to fairly distribute the available supplies.

This brings me to the reason why we always had a surplus of such a highly prized and scarce commodity as soap. By the broad brush definitions of rationing, there was only one size of cinema. Accordingly, there was only one size of soap ration. Bear in mind that in those days a bar of soap cleaned everything - floors, babies, shirt collars, etc.

So, despite being only a 300 seater rural fleapit, the soap allowance granted was the same as for the Odeon, Leicester Square and the other giants.

Helping out your friends is one thing, but when you are still left with a great surplus of what a lot of people would like to get their hands on it will not be long before some bright spark comes up with a cunning plan.

Our bright spark arrived with a checklist to detail our cinema's surpluses and deficiencies, with the result that our surplus soap was packaged up and sent of by rail to be collected at Leicester station. About a week later a similar package arrived from Leicester containing tea, sugar, butter and other good things we did not have in abundance. Thereafter, whenever a package of soap was sent away a package of groceries was returned.

This transaction became so routine that the task of collecting our inbound parcel was eventually delegated to my brother, although he was still but a schoolboy.

This went without a hitch until, trying to balance it on the handlebars of his bicycle, Dave dropped the package, which split open at the corner. The significance of the contraband was not lost on him and when a policeman helped him to lift it back up onto his bike he was terrified in case the contents burst out onto the road. He arrived home pale and shaken, but with the groceries intact.

Meat was subject to a different arrangement, this time resulting from a chance encounter on a foggy night.

My mother was standing at the garden gate, looking down the road for any sign of my father, who was late returning home. Presently she heard a wheezing sound and the fog parted to disclose the squat, unkempt figure of the village ne'er-do-well, hobbling along as fast as the large sack he was carrying would allow.

He paused at our gate and listened for sounds off. As he heard the unmistakeable crunch of boots on the path, he sighed, heaved his sack over our fence and informed my mother that she had not seen him.

As the murk closed around his departing figure, the village bobby came into view, panting out his own personal fog patch.
"Have you seen old Tommy around, missus?" he gasped, leaning on the gatepost for support.
"I'm just looking for our Bill, constable, he's very late." was the oblique reply.

The sack was later found to contain a significant quantity of pig, in kit form.

The presence of such a large quantity of meat in those days of strict rationing was quite an embarrassment and several anxious days were spent waiting for Old Tom to return for his spoils. Finally, after a week had passed with no contact from the villain, my mother decided to return the contraband to its wrongful owner. My old pram was singled out as the most suitable conveyance for the pig's journey across the village.

No issue was raised that the passenger, especially in its dismembered state, bore no great resemblance to the pram's former occupant, so the cosily blanketed pig returned home.

Tom's house was as eccentric as its owner.

Built by his own hands, it boasted solid walls, small windows and a stout roof. Its single room was kitchen, bathroom and bedroom to Tom, his wife and their numerous children. The floor was compacted earth and stunted vegetation eked out a meagre existence in those areas where the light penetrated and traffic was infrequent.

The centrepiece was a huge cook's table, ridged from years of being scrubbed and it was at this table that Tommy was seated, eating his dinner. To my mother's astonishment, the meal, meat, potatoes, vegetables and gravy, was served directly onto the table, without the inconvenience of a plate.

Old Tom viewed the return of the pig with ambivalence. 'You shouldn't have bothered, missus. I didn't expect to see him again,' he said, rounding up some stray gravy as it made its way towards the edge of the table.

'I sometimes have to get into bed with a dead pig when the bobby calls round' added Mrs Tom, 'the odd pig or two don't make much difference.

So it was that almost as much pig made the return journey home as had set out and I cannot remember a time from then until the end of meat rationing when we did not have half a pig hanging from the ceiling of the spare bedroom.

I must also mention our 'spies', as the mysterious Central European family who lived in the village came to be known. They had arrived in the late thirties, when the possibility of war was gaining momentum. They were most probably fleeing from the threat of the jackboot themselves, but allegedly exhibited some strange behaviour when enemy bombers were in the vicinity.

According to the tales, blackout curtains would come falling down when a raid was imminent and on one occasion a light was seen flashing from an upstairs window towards the darkening eastern sky. 'That silly boy was looking for bombers with his torch,' was the rather unconvincing explanation when the air raid wardens had entered the house. Using the full might of their powers, the wardens threatened to confiscate his torch batteries.

Eventually, a warden was detailed to watch the house when an alert was in progress and though the authorities were alerted, no further action was taken. They may just possibly have been spies, but if they were, they were our spies.

I can't help having doubts about these stories. Knowing the curiosity my own family aroused when we joined that very close community from only two counties away, genuine European immigrants were sure to become the source of legend.

I can't tell you much more about the war. I once saw the skies black with Dakotas pulling huge gliders, possibly practising for Arnhem. I also remember there was always a reserve Spitfire kept in the local bus company's garage, but that remained there long after the war had finished.

Of VE Day I remember nothing, but I recollect that I won sixpence on the sports day held in the village to celebrate VJ Day. This event was held on the council tip which, oddly enough, was situated in the centre of the village, where the medical centre now stands.

So it was that I saw my first bonfire and firework display and, having accepted cash for third place in my sprint, disqualified myself for the Olympics! In those far-off Corinthian days the Olympic Games were, of course, strictly for amateur competitors who had not sullied their good names by accepting even trifling sums of money for their sporting endeavours.

Soon, the only visible reminder of the war would be the rusting barbed wire on the wall of the old prisoner-of-war camp. It would take years for those tangled strands to disappear.

By the time the war had ended, I was a schoolboy, so for me a new war had begun.

"Aren't you the boy....?"

For some reason my mother did not want me to go to school in our village, so I had to walk to an identical school in the next one, Polesworth. It was down hill all the way there, but of course, was uphill all the way home.

Polesworth, situated on the River Anker, which takes the slow lane to the sea via the Tame, Trent and Humber, is celebrated as the home of the Anglo-Saxon Saint Editha and for its connection with the Tudor poet Michael Drayton.

It was there that I discovered that among the neighbouring villages natives of Dordon were known as "cuckoos", due to the apocryphal tale of the inhabitants who tried to keep a cuckoo in a field by closing the gate. I had always thought it was the wise men of Gotham who had first hit on that idea.

My first teacher was a creature of wonder - a woman who rode a motorbike! Actually, it was a moped, or autocycle as they were called in those days, but still pretty avant garde for 1945.

I remember little of my first day amid the newness and confusion of being away from home for the first time, but I do remember Neville. Nev was a farmer's son who was inconsolable for the whole of that traumatic first day. The more the unfortunate teacher tried to pacify him, the more upset he became, at one point threatening to drown the unfortunate pedagogue in a bucket of water.

Nev eventually settled in, as we all did, and he became one of my pals. When I ran into him some twenty years later he was a policeman.

My other closest mates at that time, were Billy, a quiet, almost morose character and Mike, a bright lad whose father had been killed flying Spitfires and whose wealthy mother had deposited him in the village in the care of an ancient and doting nanny.

The straight-laced old lady would turn in her grave if she knew that the large house in which she raised Michael had later been converted into a pub.

The start of my school career briefly overlapped with the end of my brother's and while it did not always suit him to acknowledge me, it did mean that in an emergency I had a defender. Mind you, I did not believe his claim to be 'cock of the school', as the head bully was known.

At first my school life was plain sailing, with my mother's pre-school education helping me to be at the top end of the class.

Unfortunately, I then made the acquaintance of the Head Master.

Tall and lean, with piercing eyes and sleek, dark hair, silvering at the temples, 'Daddy' as he was unaffectionately known, would have made a splendid Count Dracula, had Hammer Films then been invented.

Years later, he would come flooding back into my memory whenever I saw his effigy in Pink Floyd's 'Wall' video.

He had a strange, articulated body, which allowed him to lower his head like an anglepoise lamp until his sharp face and malevolent eyes floated inches from your face, picking out every pore and pustule, uncovering any untruth or secret.

By keeping my head down and not doing anything to attract his attention, it was several years before he was anything more to me than someone who spouted interminably at morning assembly - a sinister figure to be feared, certainly, but not the stuff of nightmares.

When our paths finally crossed, it was at my instigation. I went to his office to ask a favour.

My father, a lifelong motorcycle fanatic, had tickets for a flight to the Isle of Man for the

T.T. races and persuaded my mother to let me go, despite it being on a Friday, a school day. My father's logic argued that an aeroplane flight for a ten year old boy would have far more educational value than any classroom experience and so a letter to my Head Master was composed seeking permission for my absence.

My attendance at his office was commanded during break and I was ushered into his presence by his secretary, who offered me a sympathetic glance before she closed the door and sealed off my escape route. My parents' letter lay open on the desk and the Head Master picked it up and pretended he was reading it for the first time.

'Isle of Man', he mused with what he probably thought was a genial smile. 'T.T. races. Very nice'.

Good experience. Very educational. I rehearsed the answers to the questions I thought would follow. The question that did follow caught me completely off guard.

The Head's face swivelled down and stared into mine.

'You're the chap who plays the fool at the dinner table, aren't you?'

It was a rhetorical question, which was as

well, for I had never to the best of my knowledge given any cause for criticism in this area and had no idea what sin I had committed.

I mumbled a non-contradictory reply.

'Don't you think I would not prefer to fly to the Isle of Man rather than be stuck here teaching you ungrateful people?' he continued.

Despite my failure to imagine him enjoying anything that did not involve inflicting pain, I again made a placatory response.

'I'm afraid that if your parents are not concerned for your education, I am.' He was now warming to his subject and enjoying my discomfort. 'A person who wastes as much time as you do cannot expect to be granted even more.'

There was more of the same, but by now I knew that the Isle of Man was slipping below my horizon.

As I returned home that evening I did not realise that I had managed to imprint on my Head Master's mind the indelible impression that I was the evil one who acted the fool at the dinner table, that I existed for that purpose alone and that without me the dinner table would be a place of tranquillity and good fellowship.

Whenever he conversed with me after that day, which sadly became more frequent, my dinner table shortcomings, whatever they were, invariably opened the conversation.

Imagine my surprise when, on the day following my initial harrowing encounter, the Head Master announced at assembly that the school would be closed, for de-lousing or something, on the very day in question. The Isle of Man trip was on after all!

I squirmed with anxiety for the rest of that day, in case my father had called off the trip or offered my place to someone else. Happily, my fears proved unfounded and on the appointed day my father, his chief projectionist, John, and I arrived bright and early at Elmdon airport to savour the unfamiliar sights and sounds of air travel.

It was wonderful, with aircraft landing, taxying and taking off to all parts. All parts, that is, except the Isle of Man.

Our flight was a charter and no one seemed to know anything about it. Enquiries resulted in the information that the flight had been chartered by a Mr. Brown, who was clearly the man to see. At this point Mr. Brown began to get worried, learning only later that his name had been used as he was the first person to make a booking.

Eventually, by eliminating all the aircraft that had moved since we arrived, we decided that our aircraft was the antique, yellow Rapide biplane standing forlornly on the apron. A confection of wires, struts and canvas, it had at least stood the test of time, but gave off the appearance of an hastily unwrapped parcel.

Departure time had long gone when an old boy in an RAF blazer lurched unsteadily towards us, his bleary eyes peering over the bags on which they had been resting and struggled to focus.

'Are you chaps going in that yellow thing?' the apparition asked the ten of us who had by then gathered. We admitted that we were, except for one nervous little, bald man who recoiled saying, 'Oh, no. Count me out!' and retreated hastily, to become the rat leaving our sinking ship.

'I'll just see if there's any weather', said our pilot and he shuffled off to the Met Office, shoulders drooping and with a briefcase as battered as he was dangling precariously from his fingers.

He returned fifteen minutes later, minus the briefcase, muttered to himself for a while and then wandered off again for another quarter of an hour before returning with a crumpled copy of a weather report. He seemed vaguely surprised that we were still waiting but announced that he was now ready to depart.

He lurched out onto to tarmac and made his way to the aircraft. We followed on behind and looked on as he opened the flimsy, canvas covered door and climbed in.

'Last one in shut the door,' he called over his shoulder.

It must be said that the flight that followed was a sheer delight, low enough to pick out features on the ground in detail and clear enough to see for miles. Seated immediately behind the pilot, I also had a good view ahead.

It was quite disconcerting when the pilot left his seat during the flight and went rummaging around in the rear of the cabin, but I was not called upon to make an emergency landing or take evasive action, although my father had told me that this was the responsibility of the person seated immediately behind the pilot.

The lateness of our departure meant that the racing had already started by the time we arrived at Ronaldsway airport, but an high speed taxi ride soon got us to the nearest vantage point on the circuit, Braddan Bridge. There, a smiling vicar was happy to sell us seats in his churchyard from which to view the spectacle.

So it was sitting on the churchyard wall that I was able to cheer on Artie Bell to second place in his final T.T. race and was delighted when, on the last lap, my hero saw and returned my wave.

Sadly, his racing career came to a sudden end a few weeks later when he and several other riders demolished a commentary box at the Belgian Grand Prix.

After the races, we walked into Douglas town before catching a bus back to the airport. The bus, a double decker, was even faster than the taxi on this speed-mad island and John, who had been a sailor during the war, told us it reminded him of the maniac who drove their liberty bus in Portsmouth.

Sure enough, when we arrived at Ronaldsway, John leapt from the bus and was soon in animated conversation with his old shipmate.

We found the pilot in the bar, where my father bought him a drink. I did not consider this to be the wisest course of action, but Dad assured me that by this time it would make very little difference to our chances of survival.

The rest of our party drifted back in ones and twos until all were present and we followed our leader out to the little yellow biplane. As we were now used to his informality, we jumped in, shut the door and took our seats. Our complacency was soon dispelled.

'Does the port engine sound a bit rough to you?' our pilot called out to no one in particular.

No one in particular replied. He seemed encouraged by this and revved up the engines.

'We'll give it a try and stooge round for a bit and if necessary we can come back,' he added.

Thus reassured, we hurtled towards the cliff edge that marked the boundary of the airfield and of the Isle of Man. Having failed to plummet into the sea, we followed the same route as the Isle of Man Steam Packet vessels and had a great view of Liverpool docks, crammed as it was in those days with ships from all over the world.

Home at last, I was of course unaware that this was only the first of over 700 flights that fate had in store for me. It remains, however, the most magical.

Back at school, I finally arrived in a position

of seniority. I was always in the top three in examinations, was generally popular with the staff (except the aforementioned Headmaster) and was a fairly regular hero in my group as a winner of 'House Points'. So, life was pretty good.

Not perfect, of course. I envied the miners' sons big, heavy boots they received from the Miners' Welfare Association, really clumpy and far better for all practical purposes like fighting or football than my pathetically flimsy shoes.

Talking of football, the miners' kids may have got their footwear from 'the Welfare' but they all had proper football shirts. I had to make do with an ordinary shirt that had gone horribly wrong in the wash, resulting in it becoming a livid, bilious green and rendering it impossible to wear for school or best. So while the rest of my mates ran out in their claret and blue shirts, I took the field looking like a fluorescent bogey.

I was re-christened 'Snot Shirt' and firmly believe that my hopes of becoming a giant in the world of football were dealt a fatal blow by this humiliation.

After all, 'The Green Bogey' has none of the charisma of 'The Black Pearl' does it?

Then, one day I passed my eleven plus

exams. This was a rare occurrence at my school and the other successful candidate and I were viewed with some suspicion for a while, as though we had suddenly become holy. My mates were suddenly reluctant to play with me, as though football may damage my delicate brain or prove insufficiently stimulating intellectually.

The great news was broken by my old pal the Headmaster.

He entered the classroom on the fateful day with his teeth bared in what he must have thought to be a smile. 'There must be a couple of pretty proud people here this morning', he opened. We looked around us and hoped for a further clue. 'Stand up, the two of you who have passed for the Grammar School', he added.

As neither I nor the other freak had been notified of our success, we both sat tight and forced the Head to read out our names. We shuffled sheepishly to our feet, the pleasure of our success being overwhelmed by our embarrassment at being publicly unveiled.

A flicker of disappointment crossed the Head's face as he recognised me, but whether this was because his favourite whipping boy was about to elude his grasp or merely that he would have to go to the trouble of selecting a substitute I would never find out. For once my misdemeanours at the dinner table were not on the agenda. Instead, he merely congratulated us and announced that, in order to prepare us for our academic careers we two chosen ones would be given homework for the remainder of the school year.

Suddenly, it was the rest of the class who seemed to be wreathed in smiles.

Later that day I was accosted by the Deputy Head, a bull of a man in the Brian Glover mould who claimed to have played football for Bradford Park Avenue. He placed his giant paws on my shoulders and looked dolefully into my eyes. 'Well done, lad,' he said as I turned red with embarrassment and my mates giggled in the background.
'You know what this means, don't you lad?'
'Yes, sir,' I stammered, not expecting to have to elaborate.
'What?' he fired back instantly.
'I don't know, sir,' I groaned in wretched humiliation.

My mates, without my aptitude for higher education, fell about with laughter.

The last summer between passing the eleven plus and going to Grammar School was a rather remote and lonely one. My brother had by now left school and was an apprentice mechanic and my best mate Mike Smith had been repossessed by his mother and had gone to live in Leicestershire, so my long walk home from school was usually alone.

This was a contrast to my departure for school in the mornings, which coincided with my father taking the dogs for their walk. As my mother bred bulldogs, there could any number of excited animals leaping, vomiting and spraying vast amounts of spittle as they jostled for position at the gate.

When they were released they flowed onto the dirt road in front of our house like a tidal wave and then swept down the footpath which led to the next village and my school. Despite their rush and bustle, they were all exhausted within about 50 yards and were desperate to return home before they had escorted me for half a mile, but for those first few yards they would sweep away anything in their path like an avalanche.

Shunning the tarmac road which circled the hill, I took the shorter footpath which cut through pastures and cornfields, over stiles and through farm gates. Sadly, this route has long since disappeared, giving way to the housing estates that have now, in all but name, joined the two villages into one.

It was around this time that I first captained England at football.

I remember the pride with which I strode

onto the pitch alongside the Polish captain, who owned the ball. England won the toss and elected to kick off, while our opponents representing Poland/Yugoslavia/Scotland/Durham chose to defend the end where the high fence spared them the long walk to retrieve the ball.

Our international opposition was made up of the sons of miners who had been swept into our small community by the fortunes of war. Our side comprised eleven good men of yeoman stock, or to be more accurate, ten small boys and a wiry haired mongrel with the suspiciously Scottish sounding name of 'Nairn'.

Nairn didn't seem to belong to anyone in particular, but never missed our soccer internationals. He was an automatic choice, principally because he was going to get involved whether selected or not. He had a fair turn of speed, a prodigious leap and a biting tackle. He scorned positional play and followed wherever the ball led. Particularly dangerous in front of goal (either team's goal), his snapping jaws were ready to latch on to any stray face attempting to head the ball.

On this particular day, Nairn had responded to my captaincy by snouting us into an early lead. He had also reduced the opposition to ten men by means of a somewhat dubious tackle from behind and swept tirelessly from defence to attack with barely pause for a scratch. True, he had piddled on the pile of coats which served as goalposts and prevented us from adding to our lead by running between our centre forward's legs at the crucial moment, but all things considered he was well on his way to 'Dog of the Match' by the time an impromptu half time saw us slump exhausted to the ground.

Nairn paced around amongst the players, tongue lolling, impatient for the action to recommence. Why he chose to run out into the road, we would never know, but he did. In an instant and a screech of brakes, our star was extinguished.

Playing for England was never the same after that.

So my primary education came to a close. Despite my Headmaster's sudden change of heart towards me, I still felt like the chap who had acted the fool at the dinner table. This was despite the fact that my only recorded misdemeanour in all that time was the occasion when I was caught reading 'Treasure Island' when I should have been studying my seven times tables.

After leaving for Grammar School, I never once re-entered those school gates and while I concede that his treatment did me no permanent harm, I must confess that wain ropes and oxen would not drag me back to that accursed place and my worst nightmares are those in which I see again that old pedagogue and hear his parrot cry ringing in my ears 'Seven times eight, seven times eight'.

There's no business like show business

By the time I was old enough to appreciate the medium of cinema, my father owned a 298 seater, single level auditorium which, despite clearly having been built to a tight budget, had excellent projection characteristics and was one of the few cinemas that, many years later, was able to convert to a full Cinemascope format without losing any screen height.

From an early age, seat E1 in the front row of the most expensive seats (1/9d bookable at 2/3d), was mine unless the house was full, in which case I was unceremoniously hauled out and relocated on a radiator in the side aisle. This meant that I watched all the most popular films looking sideways over my right shoulder.

My mother's domain was the box office, where her wizardry with cash could be put to best use. Her party piece was to have someone drop a handful of coins onto the stone floor in the entrance hall whereupon she would estimate the total value from the sound of them hitting the floor. She was seldom wrong.

My father ran the business end, booking the films, advertising, maintaining the building, etc, while my brother took over as Chief Projectionist when he returned from his military service.

From an early age I helped in the operating box, sold sweets and ice cream, very occasionally was allowed to sell or tear tickets and was always a member of the non-stop cleaning and boiler room staff.

The really busy day was Saturday, the one day when even my father, who normally compensated for his late working hours by sleeping well into the morning, was out and about early.

The first task would be to sort through the packages from the British Cinema Printing Company, Burnley, Lancs., to locate the advertising posters for the following week's films. Then they were folded to fit into a large satchel and a large pot of poster paste was mixed.

When all was ready, my father would wheel out his motorcycle and we would tour the outlying villages to spread the word of the coming week's wonders.

At some places it was simple, such as handing in the poster at a shop to be pinned up in the window. At others it was more difficult, such as squelching through the mud of a pig pen to climb onto the sty roof to paste a poster to the wall of a roadside barn.

That site was my particular dislike, since I not only fell full length into whatever that greeny brown goo that pigs floor their pens with, but I was chased by a rather ill-tempered porker who either did not like the movies or resented my swimming in his garden.

Our circular tour of the villages was planned to avoid retracing our steps. An exception was the village of Birchmoor, where the road became a track and then petered out completely. This isolated community provided us with one of our more interesting locations.

The poster was pasted on the wall outside the small general store. Inside the shop there were no goods on or in front of the counter, but the stock was piled on neat shelves which rose almost to the ceiling. The shopkeeper, Herbert Merklew, was totally blind, but knew unerringly where every item was stored. When I went into the shop to leave the free cinema pass which was the reward for allowing us to use his wall (what a great prize for a blind man) I was always amazed at the speed with which the tiny, elderly and blind man could come up with any item he had in stock.

Birchmoor had another character who gave us much more trouble.

Big Freddie was a poor simple soul, though blessed with considerable size and strength.

Unlike his counterpart in our own village, Frankie, who was a happy lad who would run errands for anyone, Freddie was a wild and unbiddable character. He had a reputation for being particularly tough on cats, one of which he had drowned in a toilet, while singing, "Ding, dong, dell, pussy's in the well." It was also rumoured that he had also forced a cat through a mangle.

I cannot verify these lurid tales, but I can confirm that he looked forward to our visits with great relish, since he enjoyed eating a freshly pasted cinema poster. This caused my father great concern, not least since the poster for our rival cinema, posted on the same wall, was never touched.

We tried everything we could think of to overcome this problem, changing the flavour of the paste and even the colour of the poster, but to no avail. We even smeared our paste onto our rivals' poster in the hope that he would at least eat both, but Freddie remained resolutely loyal to us.

Eventually, we found limited success by pasting up our poster, riding around the village a couple of times until Freddie had dined and then returning to put up another. This worked when Freddie was in no mood for dessert.

Having survived the wilds of Polesworth, Birchmoor, Warton, Freasley, Wood End, Baddesley Ensor, Grendon, etc., we would arrive back home in time for the Childrens' Matinee.

The Childrens' Matinee was an entertainment devised in Hell and consisting of non-stop writhing, squealing pandemonium, rising to a unified crescendo when some major action on the screen momentarily captured the attention of the audience. It was an occasion for hiding in obscure parts of the auditorium, particularly under the stage, letting in one's pals through the emergency exits, gluing as many half eaten toffees to the floor as possible and turning the toilets into a water park.

My primary task, being in the same age group as the audience, was to mingle with our clientele and try to maintain order. As my father put it, "Try to make sure they damage each other rather than the cinema".

My secondary function was to sell sweets and ice cream from the small kiosk. However, since there was a continuous line of customers throughout the duration of the performance, I never actually got round to attending to my principal job, which is probably the only reason I survived.

The till in the kiosk contained the stickiest coins in the world, since our customers were reluctant to part with any money that had not been clutched in hands covered in toffee goo, saliva, sticky backed plastic and other nameless abominations.

In those carefree, pre-decimal days there were many items that could be purchased for an old penny and these had to be listed for almost every customer. My favourite client was the one who, having carefully decided which item to select, would tender a pound note in payment. I knew then that I would be seeing that particular little customer another two hundred and thirty nine times during the show.

After the performance, when the steaming masses had been returned to the outside world, we had the task of readying the hall for the double Saturday evening performance. Lost and hiding children had to be located and ejected, seats had to be repaired or replaced, most of what I had sold in the kiosk had to be scraped or mopped from the floor before the entire cinema was washed and disinfected.

I actually enjoyed going round with the disinfectant spray because it meant that the worst was over and only relatively clean work was left.

Home, at last, we enjoyed a hasty meal, which by tradition consisted of sausage batches dripping with tomatoes and onions and was easily the most eagerly awaited meal of the week.

After that, father changed into his front-of-house suit for the evening show, in which my role would be that of assistant sub-projectionist, dogsbody and in the winter months, stoker. One of my dogsbody duties would be to nip out at a quiet moments to purchase a copy of the 'Sports Argus' so that I could note the scores on the staff's football pontoon competition.

So, as the second house audience drifted out, Saturdays came to an end. The staff gathered for their pay packets while I, too young to work, of course, collected my ninepence, cash in hand, without deductions. (In fairness, ninepence was my starting wage, but I did get a raise from time to time.)

My father's usually stern visage was a woefully inadequate disguise, for his love of the absurd was always present just below the surface.

Part of his front-of-house routine was to sedately circumnavigate the auditorium during the performance, an unobtrusive, reassuring management presence. Upon reaching the top left side of the hall he would be faced with the long corridor which connected to the top right gangway.

It would be clear only to me, from my strange sideways view from the radiator, that the time between him disappearing top left to reappearing top right was accomplished at anything but a sedate pace. There could be only one explanation - as soon as he disappeared from sight he must have run like the clappers to the other end. But, why?

One evening, having watched this phenomenon several times, I slipped from my makeshift seat as soon as he had passed me on his descent to the front stalls and secreted myself in the box office doorway, halfway along the rear corridor. Sure enough, I soon heard the sound of running along the corridor and peeped out to see my father running at full tilt.

He offered no explanation but as he passed me simply asked, "Are you coming, then?"

The one occasion on which he hurried for real was when there was a breakdown during a performance. Even above the whistles and boos from the audience, his tread could be heard on the stairs leading up to the projection booth.
The first time I witnessed such a mishap I was amazed to see yards of film spewing out of the projector onto the floor. I was still

more surprised when my brother Dave, who was in command of the projection room, paused during his remedial action to make the unusual comment, "Clump, clump, clump, bong, what gives?"

I was about to ask for a translation when I heard the self-same clumps followed by the bong of the teak fire door as it hit the wall. My father's head appeared in the doorway. "What gives?", he said.

Clearly, I had much to learn about the movie business.

First Innings

For me, cricket began with Donald George Bradman, who I was assured was the finest batsman who ever lived, though sadly an Australian.

For while I can remember the first F.A. Cup Final which took place during my lifetime, (probably because my father's home town team, Derby County, were the victors) I have no recollection of the summer game before the 1948 Australians came to re-assert their authority over us.

Bradman had me confused. He he was working for the downfall of old England, just like the chap with the Charlie Chaplin moustache who we had been at war with all my life, yet somehow he was regarded as a hero instead of a villain, lionised instead of ostracised.

I remember his final Test innings at the Oval. We were visiting Nottingham at the time and my father, my Uncle Stan and I were listening to the match on the radio. When England had been bowled out for 52 and the Australian openers had passed our total, my father and uncle lost interest and went outside to tinker with a motor car.

Thus to me alone was confided the news that the evil Bradman was dismissed for a 'duck'.

I ran outside to spread the word and rejoice at the downfall of our enemy, only to find my kinsmen disappointed at the sad end to a glittering career.

I wish I had been old enough to appreciate Bradman.

Cricket had long held a prominent place in my family history. In addition to my grandfather's exploits at Loughborough, my father was also a keen follower of the game. His career with Notts schoolboys came to an abrupt end after a particularly hostile spell injured two of the opposing team. His five wicket haul won him the match ball, but he was never selected again.

After all, they had a much more docile lad named Larwood waiting in the wings!

My father could not recall ever playing with Harold Larwood, but claimed to have played several times with his Notts and England partner, Bill Voce.

In her childhood, my mother also rubbed shoulders with a future Notts cricketing legend, for she used to earn pocket money by wheeling out the baby Reg Simpson in his pram.

My own playing career began in the late forties, when my father played for Freasley, in the northernmost tip of Warwickshire. Both the club and its charming little ground have long since passed into history, but it was there that I had my first taste of the game that would prove to be an enduring passion.

I would normally be there as a camp follower, of course, but occasionally a crisis would require my name in the score-book. Still more infrequently I would be required to spend some precious moments at the crease, while the tea ladies hurried to complete their preparations.

On these great occasions, I would waddle to the wicket girded with huge pads that reached my waist and wielding the smallest bat my team mates could find, still far too large for me.

I well remember my very first innings. From the boundary, the bowler had looked fearsomely fast, but when he bowled to me he produced a gentle lob. He also managed to time its arrival to coincide with the my huge, uncontrolled swing of the bat. The ball wobbled over the head of the square leg fielder and I scampered two runs whilst carrying the huge bat in both hands, in the manner of Mr Punch about to whack the policeman. That was the last ball of the over and my partner robbed me of the chance of further triumph or disaster by getting out before I could face another delivery.

Just when those far-off summers were reaching their height, I used to be packed off to Nottingham for the long school holiday and my poor Uncle Stan, almost crippled from a motorcycle accident some years before, would hobble in to bowl to me for hours on end on the Forest Fields.

My primary school had not heard of cricket and I do not remember ever seeing Freasley practice, so my tuition was down to my father, using a narrow strip of land adjoining our house. This practice strip was rutted, bumpy and circled by highly breakable things like windows. Consequently, the only shots I mastered were the Forward and Backward Defensive Strokes. This, combined with a playing surface that could make a straight ball turn like Shane Warne, enabled me to become quite difficult to bowl out.

It limited my range of attacking shots, however, and though I was awarded four runs for guiding the ball through a small hole in the wall at short extra cover, I never found a cricket ground so laid out as to enable me to capitalise on this skill. Thus, as my life entered double figures, I was able to bat for hours without scoring any runs.

It was only when I arrived at Grammar School that I began to play organised cricket with my own age group. 'Organised' is perhaps an exaggeration, since the master in charge had ceded his authority to whichever gang leader wanted to take it. Teams were selected on the basis of gang hierarchy and the few of us outside the chosen twenty-two were left to our own devices with whatever broken kit was left over.

It was on such an occasion that I was batting in the nets when the Head Boy saw me.

Now, at our school (founded in the name of good old Queen Bess back in 1572), the Head Boy had powers second only to the Headmaster and by tradition handed out punishments which would turn most of the teachers pale.

Accordingly, he was a good man to have on your side.

This particular Head Boy, Tom Angear, was a superstar. Brilliant academically, he was also captain of cricket and football and the Victor Ludorum of the track and field team.

'What's your name?' he interrupted my cover drive.
'Brown, sir'.
Don't call me 'sir'. I'm not a teacher. What house are you in?'
I thought he should have known that. He was the head of it. I told him, forgetting to remember not to call him 'sir'.
'Don't call me 'sir'. Why aren't you playing

out there?' He waved a hand in the direction of the cricket square, where the game had dissolved into its usual gang warfare.

'Wasn't picked, sir,' I mumbled. He looked scornfully to the square, where the weapons of honour were being despoiled by barbarians.

'Perhaps as well' he mused before walking off, hands in pockets, as only the Head Boy was permitted.

The following day, he sent for me.

'You will be playing in the game next week,' he told me without preamble. 'And you will be opening the batting for the 2nd XI the following Saturday. Nets Tuesday night.'

As I was a year younger than anyone else in the 2nd XI, I was stunned, but he spoke with an assurance that convinced me that this would come to pass. He was as good as his word and in Tom Angear I had found a mentor.

On the next sports afternoon, I was collared by the head of the 2nd Form Mafia. 'I've decided to let you play with the big boys today,' he lied. I smiled smugly, knowing it was a lie. 'I'm going to knock your effing head off,' he added sweetly.

That did have a ring of truth about it.

Fortunately for me, the bowlers lacked the skill to back up his threat and I had little trouble in sorting them out. The Sports Master was not in evidence and I saw no prefects in the vicinity, but word somehow got back to the Head Boy, for next time he saw me, he grinned from ear to ear.

On the following Saturday, I opened my 2nd XI career with a duck, but despite my fears I retained my place, started to put together a few runs and only left the team when I was promoted to the Firsts the following season. In those days, it was the rule that in the last few weeks before the GCEs, candidates would be omitted from school teams so they could concentrate on their studies.

Happily, the tradition did not survive to my examination year, but just long enough to allow my premature entry to the 1st XI.

As a dispensation for coming to school on Saturdays to make teas for the cricket matches, the girls were allowed to dress like people. Gone were the ankle socks and gym slips, on went the warpaint and battledress.

It so happened that my First XI debut coincided with the tea roster nominating a lass on whom my eye had been fixed for some weeks, but I was totally unprepared for her transformation into a vision.

For the second time, I celebrated a debut with a duck.

On this occasion, however, I did make some reparation. Fielding, like most newcomers, at silly mid-off, I managed to snap up three diving catches as our fast bowlers worked over our opposition's top order.

At the tea break, I watched my vision as she adroitly avoided the verbal and physical traps that my more established team-mates put in her way as she delivered plates of sandwiches and refilled teacups. She showed scant appreciation of their boasted achievements in the game in progress and was unimpressed by their bravado.

'Those catches were wonderful,' she whispered into my ear as she leaned over my shoulder to fill my teacup. Getting a duck is never enjoyable, but that one was the least painful.

I somehow held on to a place in the team for the rest of the summer, at the end of which my mentor, the Head Boy, left school for army life with the Gurkhas, where he would serve under Joanna Lumley's dad.

On the last day of term he collected the trophy for the 'Cricketer of the Year' at the valedictory assembly. As he had won the trophy before, he knew that the base was loose and took hold of both halves, thereby becoming the only recipient not to have to crawl around the stage to recover part of his award.

I don't know whether it was the perverse sense of humour of the staff or just some obscure school ritual, but the clattering of silverware around the stage on these occasions seemed to be as inevitable as some lucky winner falling down the steps in his attempt to return to the audience.

Nothing cuts an enlarged ego back down to size better than, after dropping your hard earned prize all over the stage, falling down the steps under the malevolent gaze of four hundred pairs of sadistic eyes.

One year, there were so many fallers during rehearsals that the Head Mistress of the girls' school gave a master class in the correct technique of stairmanship. A stately, elderly spinster with the glassy smile of a redundant royal, she posed elegantly at the top of the steps.

"The secret," she confided, "is to take a half turn at the top...."

She had intended to say more, but having placed one sensibly shod, half-turned foot onto the top step, she suddenly shot from top to bottom so fast that her mortar board appeared to hang suspended in mid-air until it realised that her head was no longer supporting it.

She landed at the foot of the steps with a resounding clatter, displaying more of her underwear than anyone had seen since Mafeking night.

"Go on, then", she said amid the awful silence that followed, "Have a good laugh and get it over with."

I made up my mind at that moment that when I won the 'Cricketer of the Year' I would also grasp both halves of the trophy and return to my place with the same nonchalant grace as my hero.

I owed it to him.

The Learning Curve

Going to Grammar School rendered all my previous scholastic experience obsolete. I now wore a cap and blazer and had to travel to school by bus. Sadly, the long trousers I had hoped would round off my ensemble were postponed for a year and I had to start 'big school' still wearing shorts. But these were trivialities. There were more significant changes.

I was now at the bottom of the class, not popular with the teachers, most definitely the chap who acted the fool at the dinner table and yet, for some unknown reason, could do no wrong in the eyes of the Headmaster.

This favouritism was unsought and undeserved, but was most useful on several occasions, such as the time the Head entered the school library just as I was bringing a chair down on the head of a smaller boy.

'Maintaining discipline, Brown,' beamed my mentor, 'Good show!'

The rest of the teaching staff were an assortment of weirdos, sadists and well-meaning nutters. One pair of male teachers flounced around the school together in matching outfits and this, of course, in those less enlightened days when behaviour of that kind could still be rewarded with a prison sentence. One elderly female art teacher could not keep her hands off the boys' dangly bits, a story I did not believe until my turn came around.

The Head of Mathematics believed that the best way to encourage the correct answers out of his pupils was to draw all over their faces with coloured chalks while they struggled over a problem at the blackboard. Oddly, it seldom seemed to work, but he persevered with his radical teaching method, much to the delight of those of his pupils who had not yet been victimised in this way.

The Senior French Master, a bucolic veteran who owned the most tattered and moth-eaten gown in the hemisphere, would write his comments on homework in the most totally indecipherable scribble, so that his classes ran late with the queue of wretches lining up to obtain a translation of the almost inevitable punishment.

We compiled a glossary of his more commonly used hieroglyphics and found that 'Albatross' meant 'Absolutely useless' and 'Thundery' translated as 'Thursday', ie detention night.

Even so, I had to queue for twenty minutes on one occasion to discover that his criticism was of my own handwriting!

He was so loved that one wag in our group penned some immortal lines in his honour:

> Mr Parry is sixty-two
> He doesn't like me
> And he doesn't like you.

This proved so popular that the following year a revised version was issued:

> Mr Parry is sixty-three
> He doesn't like you
> And he doesn't like me.

The list went on with a Religious Knowledge teacher who was not only an atheist but a Communist as well and a female History teacher with the build of a front row forward whose unmarried status did not surprise us, but whose subsequent pregnancy mystified even those of us who had received the immeasurable benefit of the Headmaster's sex talk. Actually, 'sex talk' is a bit of an exaggeration; he taught us how to masturbate and then told us not to do it.

There was also a one-legged Chemistry teacher who, presumably because he was slowest to flee the Staff Room when volunteers were being lined up, landed the plumb job of escorting the school football team to its away fixtures. Being a uniped was no great disadvantage to him in his Chemistry lab, but it was less than ideal for a chap in charge of a football team. It would take him ages to creak onto the team coach and even longer to get off again, while navigating up and down the touch-line to shout encouragement, instructions or abuse to his charges invariably left him at the opposite end of the pitch to the play.

The fact any such comments as were heard were delivered in a 'trouble at t'mill' type northern accent only added to the comedy element of his performance.

It was customary in those far-off days to share mugs of tea and slices of fruit cake with the opposition at the conclusion of school football matches. On one such occasion, the fruit cake at an away match proved too hard for mere human teeth to crack so, in an unprecedented bout of good manners, we spared our hosts embarrassment by secreting lumps of cake about our persons before embarking upon our coach for the homeward journey.

Sadly, our exemplary behaviour could not be maintained and there soon developed a game which involved throwing cake from the coach windows at hapless passers-by. The hilarity of this new pastime soon attracted the attention of our one-legged custodian, who looked up from his newspaper to witness a piece of missile cake rebound from the head of an innocent pedestrian.

'Driver, driver, stop this bus', commanded Hopalong, seizing the boy he suspected to be the propellant. 'You are going to apologise, young man', he informed the miscreant.

By the time he had creaked his way off the bus with his wriggling prisoner, however, the victim had resumed his journey and was several streets away. Undaunted, he accosted a similar looking pedestrian. 'Excuse, me,' he gasped.

The pedestrian turned to see a northern Long John Silver holding an unwilling Jim Hawkins by the scruff of the neck. 'Excuse me,' repeated the old sea dog, 'Have you been hit on the head by a piece of cake?' The exact reply is lost to history, but is believed to have been worthy of the occasion.

As my school career developed, my two closest pals became Neville "Nibs" Ball and Eric "Tusker" Turney, two very different characters. Nibs was a studious and intelligent seeker of knowledge, brandishing a religious fervour like a hellfire preacher from an American TV show.

An Oxbridge candidate if ever I saw one, studying came first and second on his list of preferences, with sport nowhere. Nibs and his rigorous revision schedules deserve at least as much credit as any of our teachers for whatever success Tusker and I eventually achieved in exams.

To make him endurable, he was capable of unleashing a wild sense of humour, while his generally belligerent demeanour was leavened by a love of poetry and literature.

Tusker was more like me, somewhat less interested in work and more into fun. For 'fun' do not read 'games', however, for Tusker was an epileptic and carried a note excusing him from games. Actually, he used his note wisely, reluctantly excusing himself from those activities he did not enjoy, like swimming and cross-country running, while bravely enduring those pastimes he liked, such as cricket and football.

Even as an acknowledged master at dinner table tomfoolery, I had to bow the knee to Tusker. He was the only person I have known who could remove the trousers of the unsuspecting boy sitting opposite to him at lunchtime, not always without a struggle, of course.

With all this talent, he still found time to be a skilled musician and regularly played the organ at his local church. It was only logical that Tusker's musical background and my poetic bent should be combined to form the world's worst and most unsuccessful song-writing duo.

This was probably due to the mismatch of my groovy, upbeat lyrics with his church organ based music.

Fortunately, by popular demand, none of our output has survived, but if you try singing "Great Balls of Fire" to the tune of "All things Bright and Beautiful" you will get some idea of our unique symbiosis.

It was Nibs who decided that we should rally to the cause of the Dramatic Society when they were casting around for Shakespeare fodder. He had secured the part of Charles, the wrestler, in a production of 'As you like it' and decided that Tusker and I should provide moral support as spear carriers. This was fine for Tusker, who had no lines to learn and could disrupt rehearsals with unscripted inappropriate comments. I was not so lucky, as the director decided that I was his Orlando, the leading man with yards of dialogue.

Worst of all, I had to wrestle the mighty Nibs.

To gather inspiration, the cast were packed off to Stratford to see the real thing and it did not take the heavenly Rosalind and I to detect that we were not in the same league as Peggy Ashcroft and Richard Johnson.

Nibs was fired up, however. 'That wrestling was rubbish,' he said. 'We can do much better than that!'.

True enough, it was a bit like handbags at twenty paces, but I was more worried about learning my lines and wondering how I had got myself into this mess.

Undaunted, Nibs arranged for us to have lessons in learning how to fall without incurring major injury, as well as one or two rudimentary wrestling holds and throws. Hours were spent in the gymnasium after school, when Nibs would cheerfully fling me around with little concern for either my welfare or the minor detail that I was supposed to emerge victorious from the encounter. By the time the show was ready for full rehearsals I had learned a few of my lines and how to extract my head from the wall-bars without tearing off my ears.

Rehearsals went better than expected and the stage was less painful to land on than the hard gymnasium floor.

All things being considered, the show went reasonably well, with some minor disasters lurking in the wrestling scene in Act One.

Only on opening night did I discover that one of my shoes was too large and I had to go through the performance with my foot clenched to prevent it from falling off. Needless to say, it flew away into the wings during the wrestling match, where it was neatly caught by the prompter.

The wrestling match itself went without a hitch for a couple of nights, but the end of the scene, after Orlando says something slushy about Rosalind, I was left on stage, sniffing a rose and feeling like a total prawn because the idiots backstage forgot to close the curtain.

The following night, after receiving a severe reprimand from the director, they whipped the curtain closed just as I was preparing to deliver the closing lines.

By now the wrestling was going really well and all Nibs' efforts were paying off in audience applause. Possibly we were even beginning to think it could not go wrong.

But it couldn't last and for no apparent reason the fastening on my doublet, which had to be removed for our fight, refused to unfasten. I floundered around the stage, while a couple of courtiers tugged desperately at my sleeve trying to free it. Meanwhile, Nibs ad-libbed by dancing around, shadow boxing like Rocky Marciano. After a horrendous tearing sound I was freed and the fight was pursued to its preordained conclusion. Pre-ordained, that is, until the final performance.

I had heard from Tusker that Nibs was not

too happy at having to lose all of our encounters on stage, especially as he had been largely responsible for the choreography. There had also been some pressure from neutrals for him to get a win under his belt before the week's run was over. Even so, it came as a surprise when, on the final evening, Nibs got stuck into me with unaccustomed vigour.

'Oh, excellent young man,' quoth Rosalind, as I flew through the air and landed on a pile of chairs off stage left. When the fight entered what should have been the final move I found myself back in hold number one and the fight starting over again.

'I hope you can remember the rest of my lines,' I gasped to Nibs as he crushed me in a bear-hug and I started to lose the will to win. Then I realised that Nibs was still fighting to the script, even though it was about the third time round, and he was now expecting a move from me.

I disregarded the planned move and substituted a swift kick in the nether regions before collapsing in a heap on top of him. The bemused cast took the opportunity to call a halt to the proceedings and when the courtier responded to the Duke's enquiry with 'He cannot speak, my Lord', he wasn't exaggerating.

Nibs was dragged from the stage and the play staggered on to its anti-climax.

Back in the maths lesson the following morning, even the cynical old Head of Maths was impressed. 'Some fight, that,' he said. 'Better than that milk and water effort at Stratford.'

Nibs was vindicated. He turned round and grinned at me through a swollen lip and I winked my good eye back at him.

More Play and Less Work

One unexpected bonus of being in a production of Shakespeare had been a lengthy ban on haircuts, so that we could look sufficiently hairy to pass as Elizabethans. This was a welcome contrast to the usual instructions to get our hair cut, as our flowing locks gave us a rare opportunity to express our individuality, clad as we were in the unflattering uniform of conformity.

In fact, the one item of school uniform which was coveted was a First XI football shirt. During our weekly football lessons we wore tacky, yellow and blue quartered shirts that no self respecting team would be seen dead in, but for school matches the chosen few got to wear state of the art gold and blue outfits with numbers on the backs. Those selected for Saturday's match collected their shirts on Friday and on those rare occasions I was elevated from the 2nd XI and drew the much coveted number 9 shirt, I carried it casually home in full view.

By contrast, the school cap was worn so far back on the head as to be virtually invisible from the front. Indeed, Colin Callis, the author of the famous verses about Mr. Parry, was once sentenced to punishment for being caught on duty without his cap before he retrieved it with a flourish from its hiding place within his matted locks.

The only type of official headgear with what could be remotely described as 'street credible' was the tasselled cap, awarded by the school to its heroes in the fields of football, cricket and athletics. Those who attained academic excellence got sod all, but the sports stars received public acclamation.

It may seem odd that attention to personal appearance suddenly arrived on the agenda when it had hitherto been an irksome requirement. This is because it was around this time that girls were invented, or at least, undergoing a major redesign.

We believed our tasselled caps and their evidence of prowess on the field of play made us look macho. The girls, of course, could not decide whether we looked bigger prats than those who hid their un-tasselled caps in their coiffure.

But these were early days and girls were more talked about than talked to, a confusing subject that divided my mates into those who affected disdain of all things feminine and those whose imaginary sexual encounters were reported in gory detail. I kept my own council, but reckoned that if Marilyn Monroe and Mother Teresa visited the school for a day, half my mates would claim that Marilyn was an old boot and the other half would boast that Mother Teresa fancied them. It was perhaps as well that, for the time being at least, sport remained our main physical outlet.

Needless to say, when I finally got the chance of a close encounter of the female kind, I blew it magnificently. Along with some of my peers, I had spent the idle hours in the pavilion waiting to bat observing Bryony, a girl who regularly graced the tennis courts adjacent to the cricket pitch.

There had been some egging on between us to see who could summon up the courage to chat her up. I was totally unprepared when she approached me and asked if I would partner her in a forthcoming Mixed Doubles tournament. In a turmoil of shock, disbelief and a nagging suspicion that somehow I was being set up by my mates, my spirits rose, fell and hovered before I heard myself saying that I didn't know how to play tennis. This was perfectly true, of course, but hardly the time to introduce such an irrelevance.

I kicked myself all the way home and again when I got there.

Too late, I purchased a racquet from Woollies and practised by bashing an old ball up against the garage wall. I made myself conspicuous around the tennis courts, hoping for a repechage, but with no joy. The lady in question had now another hopeful in tow and my chance was lost.

My efforts were not completely wasted, however, for I received another offer and this time I was not caught off guard.

Dorothy was not as attractive as Bryony, but she had all the same equipment, as well as the fringe benefit of being a better tennis player. In fact, she was far too good for a yokel like me, but after beating me round the court for a couple of weeks declared me adequate to partner in the tournament, albeit in a subsidiary role.

Actually, it turned out to be great fun and after an easy first round match, we caused a bit of a stir by overcoming the 2nd seeds. We finally came to grief in the semi-finals, narrowly losing to the eventual tournament winners. Dorothy seemed pleased with her efforts and I felt I had done well enough to deserve my reward.

This, sadly, turned out to be the pinnacle of my tennis career. I was invited to play the following year but on this occasion had not the benefit of a good partner to carry me, so we stumbled out of the competition in the first round.

Not that my school football career fared much better. I was in and out of a team that boasted schoolboy internationals and never secured a regular run in the 1st XI. I must admit, however, my disappointment at being dropped after scoring twice in a rare victory over Leicester City Boys, unquestionably my finest hour as a player.

The sad fact is that, apart from being gifted with a reasonably powerful shot in my right boot, my football skills were negligible. I could not head, pass, tackle or dribble. My left foot was strictly for standing on and 'reading' a game was a closed book to me.

As a result, I was usually selected to accompany the first team as a travelling reserve, thus missing a game with the 2nd XI. In those days, substitutes had not been invented, so there was little chance of me playing if all the selected eleven managed to make it off the bus without breaking a leg.

Worse still, the reserve was expected to change with the team, put on a blazer and run up and down the touch-line, waving a coloured flag like a demented railway guard, in order to be seen and totally ignored by the referee.

The only time I was grateful to be a linesman was one scary occasion when the boys unwisely accepted a challenge from the girls to play them at hockey. I hid behind my little flag as my team-mates subsided under a welter of waving hockey sticks and winced with evil satisfaction as they limped and bled to humiliating defeat.

Strangely, the older I got the less involved I became in the cinema. My mother insisted that my homework came first and my father, though not allowing football to excuse my cinema duties, did put my cricket ahead of them.

There were, of course, emergencies when it was a case of all hands to the pump, such as the night the cinema was flooded during the showing of "The Cruel Sea".

I was at home toying with my homework when I got the call to drop everything and report to the cinema a.s.a.p. Normally any excuse to avoid homework was welcome, but on this particular evening the rain was bucketing down and it was a half-mile walk to the cinema.

When I made this comment over the phone, however, my father pointed out that the rain had not escaped his notice as the auditorium was on the point of flooding. Arriving on the scene, I discovered that a storm drainpipe had burst and water was cascading into the underground boiler room, from where it was making its way up the heating pipe conduits and into the auditorium.

A quick look inside confirmed that the understage area and orchestra pit were under water and waves were lapping about three or four feet short of the front row of the unsuspecting audience.

On screen, Jack Hawkins was on the look-out for U-Boats, but I think he was over dramatising the situation.

The boiler room was a cellar about ten feet deep and accessed by an iron ladder. The boiler itself had disappeared below the waterline, which was about a foot under the top rung of the ladder.

Armed with the large coke buckets, it was necessary to bail out the water and empty it down a mercifully nearby drain. For some time it was a struggle to keep up with the inflow, but eventually progress was made and by the time Jack Hawkins said, "It's getting to be a different kind of war, Number One," the conduits were clear of water and the top of the boiler was visible.

Big brother Dave came down from the projection room to survey the scene and confirm that the audience were no longer in danger of having a foot-bath.

"OK, chiefy," he said, "Abandon ship!".

Together, Jack Hawkins and I had won the war.

For my last three summers at school I was the regular opening batsman for the cricket First XI, an honour I shared with a lad called Payne, who I thought was excellently named for his intended career as a dentist. At least he had a career in mind. Apart from some vague plan of joining the R.A.F., my own ambitions centred around the number of runs I could score.

To add a further dimension to my game, after playing on Saturdays for the school, I also turned out on Sundays for my local club, Birch Coppice. This was a National Coal Board financed team for the employees of the colliery, but a number of subscription paying outsiders were allowed to become members.

As all good colliery sides are supposed to, Birch Coppice had a wealth of fast bowlers, but few batsmen who could play a consistent innings with a straight bat which, thanks to my father's coaching, gave me my opportunity.

Even though it was only a local club side, it was up a gear from the school team and I learned a lot more about the game from my new team mates than from the sports master at school.

The wicket keeper, Jack Smith, showed me the art of clicking the heels together as the ball passed the edge of the bat, then holding up the ball in triumph. He also demonstrated the art of standing up to a slow bowler, flicking off the bail with the top of the pad and shouting, 'Well bowled!' Fortunately, the local umpires knew him well and were seldom fooled, whilst our own umpire hardly ever gave a decision in Jack's favour, whether fair means or foul were involved.

My first match for Birch Coppice was at Eynsham, near Oxford. As I had now a reputation for getting a 'duck' on debuts, it was with some trepidation that I went out to bat. Unfortunately, it was a two innings match and I managed to excel myself by getting two ducks in one day.

Luckily, I also held a blinder of a catch to dismiss the Eynsham opener, so I was able to show that I was not a complete waste of space.

The following week I had a decent innings and held one end open while a local legend called Ken Passey scored the runs that resulted in an unlikely victory.

After that, I was quite rightly shunted down to the 2nd XI for a couple of years to learn about club cricket. It also gave me the opportunity to bat, for the one and only time, with my father. He had retired from playing several years before, but could on occasion, with only token protest, be called upon to help out if the 2nd XI were short of players. We had the joy of sharing a match-saving partnership at Sheepy Magna, the little Leicestershire village where, some years later, I would set up home at the start of my married life.

The environment of Birch Coppice toughened me up. Most of the team were coal miners and were humorous, tough and fair. They played hard and drank harder. Often after away matches, I was the only one fit enough to carry the team kit-bag back to the coach, while the rest were singing of monks, lobsters, wild west shows, wondrous machines and the perpetually tardy Mr. Banglestein.

On one occasion, after only partially stopping an edge through slips, I noticed that the little finger on my left hand was bent back at a totally unacceptable angle, with blood flowing and a whitish thing that looked remarkably like bone sticking out.

To me this looked horrendous, but to my coal miner mates it was normal and anyone who had a full set of fingers was looked upon with grave suspicion. The batsman who had done the damage examined his handiwork briefly before yanking my fingers back into place. I screamed inwardly and my captain sent me to get my hand bandaged, reminding me to be quick, as we had no 12th man.

My big break at Birch Coppice came when injuries deprived the 1st XI of both opening batsman and as I was then regularly opening for the 2nds, I was called upon to face the new ball. At 53 for 9, I was still hanging in there, but things did not look too promising, especially as the number 11 was also a schoolboy, even younger than me.

He stuck around, however, and we added 74 for the last wicket, the innings only coming to a close when I found myself in the nervous nineties and got myself out.

We won the match and were hailed as heroes and in my fifteen years with the club, I was never again demoted to the 2nd XI.

Mixed between elation and disappointment at missing out on a century, I was consoled by my team-mates. 'Don't worry', they said. 'You'll soon get one.'

Little did I know then that my maiden century in adult cricket would be scored to the cheers of a teenage daughter whose mother I would not even meet for several years.

Meanwhile, back in the classroom, I should perhaps mention that a certain amount of school work was unavoidable, augmented as it was by crippling amounts of homework.

The old School Certificates had recently been replaced by the GCEs and we struggled, helped by some teachers, hindered by others, to reach the required standards in Latin, History, Algebra, etc.
In the 'helped' category must go the Latin Master, who dragged me, kicking and screaming, to the most marginal of 'O' levels.

When, at the beginning of my 6th Form year, I decided to grace the 'A' level Latin class with my presence during a free study period, the frantic teacher refused to let me into the room, fearing that I planned to participate.

In the 'hindered' category went the History Master, who banned me from lessons during the pre-exam term because of a dispute in the dining room, where I led a revolution by a group of renegades who held the outrageous view that fifteen-year-olds are mature enough to know whether they wish to eat their puddings or not. It may be hard to believe now, but in those far-off days, kids were only kids and girls wore gym-slips until they were sixteen.

This particular feud dragged on for three weeks before my old mate the Headmaster sent for me and expressed his concern that my exam result could be adversely affected. I politely rejected his suggestion that I apologise to the teacher.

'I suppose it's a matter of principle, is it,' he asked wearily. I nodded. The old school was good at supplying principles when they were needed.

'Go to your next History lesson,' he said, 'Your teacher will say no more about it.' I did and he didn't.

I also fell foul of Hopalong (he of the cake throwing episode) for my experiment called *'What happens when you attach the rubber tubing from a Bunsen burner to the water tap, put the other end into the back pocket of the boy in front and turn on the tap?'*. The answer is that you get a ban from Chemistry for the remainder of your school career.

Apart from a few other minor brushes with authority, I got through school with as little trouble and as little effort as possible. I submitted a few poems for the school magazine, did the odd play or poetry reading and occasionally got picked for the soccer 1st XI.

Other than that, I kept my head down.

Final Fling

As our school careers were drawing to a close, Tusker and I decided to spend our final Easter holiday in the Lake District. This was partly to commune with nature and partly because a party of the more delectable 6th Form girls were heading in the same direction.

Nibs refused our invitation as it was far too near to the G.C.E. exams and girls were not yet on his agenda.

Unfortunately, the girls were well chaperoned and not the soft targets we had hoped.

So it was that, despite the Arctic conditions prevailing in that vicinity over Easter, Tusker and I found ourselves footslogging across the fells and reviving ourselves afterwards in the Brown Owl's Tearooms in Keswick.

On one of our excursions we came across Mumtaz, a Pakistani lad who had come to Britain to go to university and was whiling away the vacation by freezing to death on the side of Helvellyn. He was huddling in the shelter of a rough stone wall and looked so miserable that Tusker felt obliged to offer him a sip of his precious Dandelion and Burdock.

The stranger eyed the sludgy brown liquid with suspicion before sampling the delicacy.

"Mmmm," he said appreciatively, "Quite wet."

Despite this introduction, Mumtaz immediately joined forces with us and the three of us set off on the following morning to climb Scafell Pike.

It was cold and rainy as we tramped through Seathwaite and the last vestiges of civilisation were left behind. At the last habitation we passed, a notice on the wall advertised meals and we stopped to ask what time they closed, so that we could get something to eat on our way back through the valley.

Two old ladies answered the door, although one of them remained partially hidden in the background. They told us that they closed at dusk, but if they knew we were going to call they would leave a lantern in the porch. We promised to return and set off into the hills.

We were not too concerned when, about an hour later, a few feathery flames of snow started to swirl around in the wind. If anything, it felt slightly warmer.

But halfway across a boggy plateau the serious snow started, driven by a biting wind that made our eyes stream. Soon it was impossible to see anything beyond the snow hurtling almost horizontally across our line of march. We circled the edge of a tarn, sought shelter in the lea of an outcrop and polished off our coffee and sandwiches while waiting for the storm to abate.

Eventually, with the storm showing no sign of passing over, we consulted the soggy remains of our map and decided to head in a straight line towards the nearest road. This was a mistake, for what looked like a straight line on the map turned out to be a very wiggly line when it came to going up and down.

We had to scramble down what looked suspiciously like a cliff before losing one of our rucksacks in the torrent that was raging through to ravine at the bottom. Tusker looked on in despair as the last of the Dandelion and Burdock was carried away downstream. Mumtaz, who had dropped the rucksack volunteered to try to retrieve it but looked relieved when no one took him up on his offer.

After stumbling around for another hour or so as darkness fell, we eventually found ourselves below the snow line and finally came across a well-trodden path. After some debate as to which direction to follow it, we had some good fortune, as we had followed it for only a few hundred yards when we saw a light ahead. It was a lantern hanging in a porch.

"Good. They're still open," said Tusker.
"We can't go in there at this time of night", protested Mumtaz, but Tusker was already hammering on the door. The door creaked open and the two old ladies, in line astern just as before, peered out and then ushered us inside.

We were led into a large, square low-ceilinged room which was lit partly by lantern and partly by the contents of a huge fireplace. The centre of the room was dominated by a stout, scrubbed wooden table, the legs of which appeared to be bending under the weight of the food upon it.

This bounty was soon supplemented by a large pot of tea and the three of us needed no second invitation to sit and eat.

Mumtaz, who much earlier in the day had told us of the foods he was and was not allowed to eat, threw all his inhibitions aside and, like Tusker and myself, ate everything put in front of him.

The silent sister did not enter the room but stood, partly hidden by the door, scurrying off to report when the teapot was empty or a tray of food needed replenishing.

Later, full to the brim and warmed to the bone, we sat back and watched the fire throw shadow pictures on the walls as our socks steamed dry on the hearth.

At last, way past the old ladies' bed time, we got up to leave. The price the sisters charged for our feast was a joke. We paid them twice as much as they asked and still felt we had robbed them, but they would take no more.

"I wish they ran the Brown Owl's Tearoom", said Tusker.

With all the fickleness of the Lake District weather, it was now a fine, clear night and so peaceful that the only sound was the crunch of our boots on the road. We walked through the remainder of the night back to town, a distance which had seemed so much shorter on the bus when we made the outward journey. With the sunrise we were only a couple of miles from our goal and our spirits were so high that when we were finally offered a lift by an early morning lorry we actually had a lively discussion over whether to accept it or not.

To our great surprise, the girls had missed us. So much so that they had alerted the Mountain Rescue Service. As a result they scolded Tusker and I for our irresponsibility and sent us off to the Police Station to apologise while they comforted poor Mumtaz after his ordeal.

We were quite well behaved for the remainder of the trip, wandering around the town or loafing in the tearooms. Mumtaz was reading a dog-eared copy of 'Wind in the Willows' he had picked up in the Brown Owl's. "I'd like to read all of this, one of these days," he said as a few more pages fell out and slithered across the floor.

When we shook hands with him at the railway station, Tusker and I presented him with a new copy.

"I will treasure this", he said. He paused before climbing onto his train. "I also promise never to drink Dandelion and Burdock ever again!"

Spring gave way to Summer and the school First XI embarked upon a highly successful season. Most of our opponents were put to the sword, our main opponents being the grammar schools of Tamworth, Coleshill, Lutterworth, Hinckley and Market Bosworth.

The match against Dixie Grammar School at Bosworth was especially popular, as it was by tradition played on a Wednesday rather than a Saturday, thus granting an afternoon's absence to the lucky participants.

In that all-conquering summer we even

managed to tie our annual fixture with the town cricket club, but as their man of the match was an old boy of the school, we counted that as a moral victory, too.

Exams came and went, with possibly less attention than they deserved, the summer was warm and pleasant, I scored a pile of runs and Grace, the girl who had encouraged me when I failed to trouble on my debut, was even more encouraging when I did score.

In due course, I won my second tasselled cap, or 'colours', as they were rather grandly called, and ultimately achieved the prize I had long coveted, the 'Cricketer of the Year' trophy.

"For it's not for the sake of a ribboned coat nor the selfish hope of a season's fame...." Not much, it's not!

On the last day of the Summer term, I climbed the steps to the stage with the same studied nonchalance that had so inspired me, accepted the trophy carefully, making sure that I had a hand on each half and with a half-turn at the top of the steps, safely negotiated my way back to my seat.

As the applause faded to an end, so did my school days, although there were exams and even some studying still to come.

Nibs went on to Oxford, as everyone knew he would. I joined him there in due course, but only for a riotous weekend in an unfamiliar city that I would get to know so well many years later.

After losing contact for a few years, Nibs and I met by chance in a lift in Liverpool, just in time for me to invite him and his new wife to my wedding in Birmingham a few weeks later.

Some years after that, while I was commuting between the Midlands and Prestwick, I stayed with Nibs and his wife, Betty, at their home in Carlisle, but sadly lost touch again in the mid-seventies.

When I did finally manage to track him down it was, sadly, only to read his obituary in his Oxford College magazine.

Tragically, Tusker did not live to see his twenty-first birthday, suffocating during one of his increasingly infrequent epileptic fits. I only heard the news a week after his funeral, when it came up casually in conversation with a fellow student who lived nearby. I visited the Church where he used to play the organ and stood indecisively at the end of the drive to his parents' home, before deciding not to call.

They would not want to know that, if there is

a heaven, the inmates had better hold onto their trousers at lunchtime.

I hope they have a good stock of Dandelion and Burdock up there, too.

Grounded

The course of our lives can be changed in an instant. Sometimes we can see the metamorphosis coming, as in the case of marriage or the imminent birth of a child. But sometimes the change can come with the suddenness of carelessly stepping off the pavement in front of a bus.

Sitting on my Piccadilly Line train as it sped eastwards towards Hornchurch and the R.A.F Aircrew Selection Centre, I had the overwhelming feeling that my life was going to suddenly remain very much as it was.

I knew I had the necessary youth, educational qualifications and the fitness of a regular sportsman, but I was also aware that my last year of school had taken the edge off my eyesight and though good enough for day-to-day purposes, I feared that it may not be up to the exacting standards the peacetime Air Force could demand of those to whom it entrusted its Meteors, Hunters and Canberras.

However, as I waited outside Hornchurch tube station waiting for the R.A.F. bus, I found myself amongst a group of lads very much like me, too loud and jocular, covering their doubts.

Those few days at Hornchurch turned out to be my only experience of military life; being roused at some unearthly hour by a Flight Sergeant tipping your bed over before returning to fling your tidily stowed bedding all over the barrack room and sending you off to queue for a breakfast that looked vaguely familiar without tasting like it.

The tests, medical, physical and mental were actually quite interesting and certainly filled our days. But my session with the opticians confirmed my fears and when at the end of the course I was interviewed by the officer in charge it was to be advised that, while the R.A.F. did consider me suitable to be offered training for a commission, it would not be in General Duties, as they categorised flying.

He went on to describe the many non-flying opportunities opening up in the service but I made it clear that if I was not suitable for aircrew I did not wish to have anything to do with aircraft.

In the light of my subsequent career, which involved over a quarter of a century in the airfreight business, that was a fairly stupid comment.

I returned home with the result I had expected and aware that, despite my anticipation of failure, I had absolutely no idea what I would do for a living. I had dreamed only of flying and now had to come up with a Plan B.

There had been a time when my father had considered buying a second cinema and using the different but complementary skills of his two sons to run it, but the rapid expansion of television had quickly created a situation where his existing cinema was struggling to survive.

It was my father that suggested accountancy might be the future for me and when he learned that his own accountant had a vacancy for an articled clerk, arranged for me to have an interview.

So it was that I drifted into accountancy and the mixed environment of working in the practice or out on audit during the day, studying at home during the evenings and attending lectures at Birmingham University on Saturday mornings.

I did, of course, receive pay, but as the amount totalled slightly less than my bus fares to and from the office in Nuneaton, I was still financially dependent on my parents.

I stuck it out for two and a half years, but deep down knew from an early stage that this was not for me.

It was by no means all gloom and doom, however. The other articled clerks were a great bunch of lads. Several of us played in the same football team and as our work place was a remote attic reached only by a very squeaky staircase, giving early warning of the approach of strangers, it must be conceded that everything that went on there could not be described as work.

On one occasion, when Attic A was playing Attic B at cricket the staircase squeaked in time to allow us to hide the bat (a ruler) and ball (screwed up paper) and resume an attitude of work at our desks before the door opened.

Unfortunately, the last shot played had hit the light fitting so that, when the boss put his head round the door, while he could see us all bent studiously over desks, he could also see the light fitting swinging wildly back and forth.

He clearly had forgotten the reason for his visit, since he simply shook his head sadly and went back downstairs.

Because all the articled clerks were skint, we formed a syndicate to report the football matches in the local league for Nuneaton's Saturday evening sports edition, which highlighted Nuneaton Borough, Nuneaton RFC, Coventry City and Leicester City, as well as the amateur leagues in the area.

In order to make the pay worthwhile it was necessary for us to report up three matches each, most of which were being played simultaneously. This involved some clever planning, high speed cycling, and a considerable amount of input from the spectators.

It was good fun in decent weather, but on rainy Saturday afternoons it was not such a good idea.

I remember one bleak midwinter's day I cycled through the snow, happy that all but one of my matches had been postponed and looking forward to reporting a match I had actually seen.

Unfortunately, more snow during the match caused this game, too, to be called off just before half-time.

I found a telephone box to notify the newspaper and was surprised to be asked for a full blow by blow report of the match up to the point of the abandonment.

As luck would have it, there had been plenty of incidents, a few goals, a sending-off and a hotly disputed penalty, so I was able to oblige with a fairly detailed account. I was then somewhat puzzled to be asked to go over each of the incidents in greater detail.

It was only when I purchase a copy of the paper that evening that I discovered Coventry

City's match had also fallen foul of the weather, resulting in me having the whole back page to myself

Although I was still registered as a player with one of the clubs in the league, I had given up playing to report for the newspaper and it was when I was allocated a match involving my former club that I had one last, surprise chance for glory.

Due to some traffic mishap, four players from my former club had failed to arrive for an away match. The reserve player was put into the line-up, as was a junior member who had already played that morning for the youth team, while a regular player who had just had four teeth out under gas was still too befuddled to refuse to play!

That still left them a man short, until I was foolish enough to poke my head round the dressing room door.

Minutes later, I was trotting onto the pitch in ill-fitting, borrowed kit to join the fun.

It was hardly surprising that our makeshift side was soon two goals down, but we were seething when just before half-time a third goal was added. What got us so fired up was the fact that the ball had not crossed the line and we felt robbed.

The second half was a revelation. My old schoolmate, Dave Hodgkins, scored twice before I had the good fortune to snatch the equaliser and then, in the dying moments completed our resurgence with the winning goal.

We were still firmly anchored at the bottom of the league but had beaten one of the leaders. I couldn't wait to read my report!

Off the field, I was wondering whether to give up on accountancy, particularly as my father was also having to review his own options, with the cinema struggling to break even.

Before the cinema finally closed, however, it did have a final humiliation in store for me.

My fellow students decided to invite themselves to a conducted tour, a free show and, as I discovered later, a free fish and chip supper afterwards.

The tour went without a hitch and we settled into our reserved seats to watch a double feature programme which teamed up an outer space adventure with an Arabian Nights type production about Omar Khayyam.

Earlier, in the projection booth, I had demonstrated the way in which the reels of film were changed without interruption by switching from one projector to another. Now I was asked to point out this phenomenon to my colleagues as it happened on screen.

"Any time now", I whispered to my group as the first set of dots warned the projectionist to start the second projector. "Watch the top right hand corner of the screen".

When the second set of dots appeared, the demonstration was complete. "There," I said knowingly, "That's all there is to it".

My smugness dropped like a lead weight to the pit of my stomach, while my so-called friends howled with delight. Where an instant before space suited heroes were treading some alien planet, the screen was suddenly filled with the Sultan's dancing girls slithering exotically across the harem floor.

"I've never seen that happen before", I croaked truthfully, though it had haunted my worst nightmares. I silently condemned my projectionist brother to a long and lingering death.

He was almost immediately granted an unconditional pardon as the camera tracked back to show that the crew of the space ship were watching a movie, but for me the damage was done.

I had been tested to destruction and would

thenceforth be known to my fellow students as 'Omar'.

Shortly after this escapade, my father announced that the cinema would be closed on Mondays, Tuesdays and Wednesdays, in the hope that the income for half the week would be more than half the income of a full week.

"And if that's a success", he added brightly, "I'll close the other half of the week, as well!"

It was and he did, without a backward glance at the industry he had worked in for over half a century.

To Cincinnati and beyond!

It turned out to be a good thing for me that while I dithered over whether or not to call a halt to my fitful accountancy studies, one of the partners called me in to his office and made my mind up for me.

It was meant to be a pep talk but actually just dislodged me from the fence. He told me that while he considered I had the ability to qualify he doubted my desire to do so.

We were in agreement. I handed in my notice the following week. As my pay was still less than my bus fares, it did not seem much point to wait until I had found another job.

I have often wondered, as I had so enjoyed my part-time job with the newspaper, why it never occurred to me to ask them if they had any full-time vacancies, but it didn't.

Meanwhile, following the closure of the cinema, my father had got a job with an automotive parts manufacturer in Birmingham. While on this occasion he wisely refused to put in a good word for me, he did give me a lift in with him so that I could try my luck with them and the neighbouring factories.

I failed to impress his employers but did secure a post at the company next door,

Cincinnati Milling Machines. I don't remember much about the interview, though it involved the Personnel Manager, the Cost Office Manager and finally, the Company Secretary.

The latter, having decided I was worth a chance, asked me, "Can you start at eight?"

At some time during the previous couple of hours I had been told that the working hours were 9 to 5 Monday to Thursday and 9 to 4.30 on Fridays, so I said, "I thought it was nine".

The Company Secretary thought for a while and then replied, "I can't start you at more than £8 10 s a week."

I hadn't even started the job and had inadvertently negotiated a ten bob pay rise already. I had finally joined the real world!

It had been my plan to hitch a lift into work with my father, but soon discovered that our working hours made this impossible and had to make my own way there. This involved a bus ride, train journey and long walk each morning. It was only two bus rides in the evenings, but with a timetable neatly constructed so that I could often see my connection pulling away as my first bus neared the stop.

This prompted me to get my own transport, first a motorcycle and then, after I had written it off with only minor personal injuries, a car.

At Cincinnati, being considered too old at twenty to taken on as a trainee and thereby inheriting all the most menial tasks, I was taken on as a clerk in the Cost Office, checking that the cost of production of the machinery was within the required parameters. I was, however, soon transferred on a temporary basis to the Import Section pending the hiring of a replacement for the previous incumbent.

I remained there for six years.

I became immersed in the world of shipping and forwarding with its Bills of Lading, air waybills, Customs Tariff and a variety of import documentation.

I really enjoyed it, with its added bonus of trips to the local airport and even to Liverpool docks, where most of our heavy ocean freight was landed.

I made myself a bit of a hero by switching the company on to around £30,000 per year they were losing in unclaimed drawback of duties on imported goods that were subsequently exported as part of completed machines.

Previously the company had only claimed on major components, but I was able to show that for the cost of an additional clerk and a dozen ring-binders, far more duty could be recovered.

I got the ring-binders, a small salary increase, unlimited overtime and the instruction to work on Saturday mornings to verify our claims with our Customs Officer.

In this way I learned that no good deed goes unpunished.

One fortunate spin-off was that my father also worked on Saturday mornings, so we would meet up for lunch before heading off to nearby Villa Park for our afternoon's entertainment.

It was at Cincinnati that I met Ellen, one of a phalanx of comptometer operators ruled over by an unpleasant and loquacious dragon, an untidily wrapped bundle of viperous affectation who fauned to the management and exercised her spleen on all of lower rank. She was not universally popular.

Ellen wisely seized an opportunity to escape into the main Accounts Department where all she had to worry about was the cynical humour of Mac, the elderly Assistant Company Secretary and the weird Welsh bloke who was in charge of imports.

I eventually managed to convince her I was not Welsh, but I think the jury is still out on the weird bit.

The reporting senior of Mac and myself was the Company Secretary, a cockney barrow boy of a man who was a treasure trove of mannerisms. One of my favourites was the way he snapped his fingers to flick the ash off his perpetual cigarette.

His office was a glass fronted box immediately behind the desks of Mac and myself. This meant that when he was in residence, which was mercifully infrequent, he had a grandstand view of our every move.

He had several desks in his office, all cluttered with paperwork, and he used to whizz from one desk to another by propelling his chair at high speed across the floor.
On one occasion, he invited me to use his office in his absence, so that I could use some of his files to work out how to import a $150,000 roll grinding machine as a trade sample, thus avoiding Customs duty of around £7,000.

Needless to say, I immediately set to entertaining my mates, Mike Hodges, Alan Pettit and Graham Godwin, fellow Accounts Department detainees beyond the glass partition, flicking ash from my imaginary cigarette, tapping the window with a ruler in imitation of our boss summoning someone to his presence and running the gamut of his mannerisms.

The climax of my performance was to whizz his chair from one desk to another. Unfortunately, I failed to appreciate just how well oiled his kept his castors, for unlike the sluggish screech of our own pale imitations, his chair took off like a racehorse. I shot across the floor in one mighty thrust, crashed into a desk on the opposite side of the office, was jettisoned under it and held firmly in place by the rogue chair, which had overturned and followed me into my dungeon.

I remained pinioned there until my mates, incontinent with laughter, finally came to my rescue.

My own chair was not nearly so skittish and it was quite usual for me to rock back on my castors, especially when engaged in lengthy phone conversations with our shipping agent in Liverpool.

To compensate my boss for missing my performance in his office, I treated him and some of his guests to an exhibition on my chairmanship for which he had a ringside seat.

Not noticing he had entered his den with

some business associates, I was on the phone to our agents in my usual relaxed manner when the two normally docile castors still in contact with the floor decided to be somewhere else and sped away, leaving me lying on my back with my legs thrashing around in the air like a fly on a window sill.

When I looked up, my gaze was met by my boss and his visitors, who had all leaned forward to peer over the edge of his desk for a better view of my downfall.

The annual audit provided us with twenty-one consecutive days work without a halt, but outside those frenetic three weeks the boys in the department usually had some out-of-hours activities together, forming our own surprisingly successful football team, going on a mercifully forgetful holiday to Wales and even, for some long forgotten reason, taking an unhealthy interest in the feats of Oldham Athletic F.C., not exactly local to we Midlanders, to the point of actually going to watch them play, though only once.

So the months and years sped by, oiled by the lunch time flickpenny league, inter-departmental cricket competition and the pleasant diversions of the in-house cinema and theatre clubs. A major high point came when our football team won a cup competition in the Birmingham Festival League. The secret of our success was that I remained on the subs bench for the whole of the final.

The Accounts Department boys also broke into the movie business and with Mike, Graham, Alan and another mate called Barry Hemmings, I made an 8mm extravaganza. Shot in the office, the empty house that Graham had just bought and down some country lane near Dordon, it was meant to be an avant garde comedy.

In fact it was so avant garde, I watched it recently and even fifty years later it still isn't funny yet. The only real comedy moments were those featuring arch-giggler Mike trying to keep a straight face.

Maybe it will be funny in another fifty years.

As the boys in the department went guilelessly on their way, the girls gradually picked them off one by one, to make them their own, so that Graham, Mike, Alan P. and Alan B. morphed seamlessly into Graham and Margaret, Mike and Maureen, Alan P. and Carole and Alan B. and Ellen.

They say that time flies when you are having fun, but even for a fun loving character like myself, six years of this kind of nonsense is more than enough.

True, I had followed my father onto the

Parish Council and was also appointed as a governor of the village school, where I had the strange experience of interviewing one of my own former teachers for the Headmaster's job. (He didn't get it.)

Even so, I was still cruising fairly aimlessly through life and it came as a surprise when I unexpectedly received an opportunity to make a complete change of career.

One of my contacts in the airfreight industry invited me to come along for an interview for a job.

The interview itself was no problem as I knew the interviewer well and a job offer seemed a formality, but company policy dictated that I also had to take the "Sales Aptitude Test", a day long torture session created by the famed Stamford Research Institute, ostensibly to identify suitable candidates, but actually to discover how many stupid questions anyone desperate for a job was prepared to endure.

The day consisted of questions like "If you had to choose, would you go out for an evening with a beautiful woman or help out a friend in need?" Actually, being one who believes that a friend in need is a pain in the neck, that was one of the easier ones, but all the questions left you feeling that whatever reply you gave was wrong.

There were also little shapes that had to be matched in pairs and questions requiring the next item in a sequence, for example, "What follows pencil, caterpillar, lasagne, dungarees, --------- ? My answer was "Waste Paper Basket", but I never found out if that was correct.

My only company during this long day was the office secretary, who handed me the papers, timed the ones that had a limit and mercifully, occasionally provided coffee.

Around 5pm, after handing me the final set of papers, she put on her coat and said, "When you have finished, leave leave the papers on the desk and I'll collect them in the morning. Turn out the light and drop the latch when you leave."

With that, she departed into the murk of a February evening.

I toiled on and completed the test and let myself out, as requested. As I stepped into the corridor of the five floor office building, I found myself in complete darkness. With the offices all around the outside of the building. the corridor had no windows and the lights had been turned off.

Unfamiliar with the building and uncertain even of which floor I was on, I had to feel my way around the walls until I arrived at the lift.

Eventually, I made to the ground floor, where I could gaze through the great glass doors at the free people of Birmingham, promenading up and down Corporation Street in the crisp winter evening. But I still could not get out.

I finally managed to burst to freedom through a fire door at the rear of the building.

I had arranged to meet Ellen to see Richard Burton and Elizabeth Taylor in "Cleopatra" and was already well behind time. When you add to that the twenty minutes the police detained me when claiming I had gone through a red light, you may appreciate that I did not see too much of the movie.

All this left me in a somewhat pessimistic frame of mind, so it was a major surprise to be told that I was the first person in years to complete, let alone pass, the Aptitude Test.

So it was that in 1966, I had to make some serious choices. I had entered my second quarter century, Ellen and I were due to marry and I had been presented with a opportunity to escape from the rut into which I was beginning to feel all too comfortable.

Unusually for me, I had no hesitation in leaping at the chance, despite that fact that I was being hired as a salesman, a role I had not filled since selling sweets at the Saturday morning childrens' matinees at the cinema.

Now I would be selling airfreight, an intangible commodity, to a similarly demanding, if less sticky, clientele.

So it was that I joined Emery Air Freight Corporation, who would be my employer for the next twenty years and change my life beyond recognition.

The Little Hut on the Canal Bank

I started work for Emery after the Easter holiday in 1966.

Although I was hired because the Birmingham Office was about to be developed from a Sales Office to a fully operational depot, I started my duties based in the same city centre building from which I had escaped after taking my aptitude test.

The one small room housed my boss, Norman, the secretary, Gill, and me.

Whilst it was the start of a journey that would take me to the far corners of North America and throughout Western Europe, my first trip was of more modest proportions, from central Birmingham to exotic Aston. As I had one day in the office before going to Heathrow for two weeks training, my new boss, Norman, felt I should get a sales call under my belt and lent me his car for the purpose.

It was not an auspicious start. I had a puncture on the way and returned to the office and hour later, covered in grease and having missed the call.

I found company cars took a bit of getting used to. When I had completed my training at Heathrow, I was presented with my own, a new Ford Anglia, almost identical to the one

I had purchased just before being approached by Emery. The main difference was that in the new car, when I pressed the windscreen washer button, water was squirted into my lap!

It proved to be a temperamental beast and the sight of Ellen and I pushing it around rural Leicestershire became a minor tourist attraction.

My sales territory was nominally the East Midlands, including Leicester, Nottingham and Derby, but Norman proved to be an unpredictable, if affable, leader whose forceful personality could open doors closed to me, while antagonising other customers with whom I was able to get along, so the geographical boundaries became blurred through necessity.

It was also not unknown for Norman to get me to cancel my plans and rush into the office, only to discover that I had been summoned only to stand in for one of his golfing partners who had cried off.

Gill was a very pleasant girl, hired at the same time as me, and preoccupied with daydreaming about her boyfriend, which left her with a very limited attention span for anything else.

I once phoned in from a customer in

Sandiacre (Notts) only for Gill to tell Norman I was in San Diego.

Norman could sometimes be work, work, work, but at other times he could seem to be bent on preventing it.

On one occasion, Gill and I had been working on a sales presentation and just returned from a quick lunch at the nearby Chinese when Norman came bounding into the office.

"How about some lunch?" he said.
"Just had some, Norm." I replied.
"What about you?" he asked Gill.
"Me, too." she replied.
"Well, then, let's just get some soup. You can manage a bowl of soup."
"We've got this presentation to finish, Norm."
"Ten minutes." said Norman. "Get your coats."
He threw me my jacket and we loyally followed him through the door.
Why he chose the local Polish Community Centre I do not know. Perhaps their soup was renowned.

You would have thought it would be difficult to find a cafeteria in central Birmingham where neither staff nor customers could speak English, but Norman managed it.

The menu was chalked up on a blackboard and Norman pointed to what he obviously thought looked like soup

"Three of them, please" he said, holding up three fingers to emphasise the point.

What arrived were three meat loaves wrapped in cabbage leaves, with potatoes, vegetables and gravy. When I say three, I mean three each!

Norman tucked in, I poked tentatively at the cabbage parcels and Gill looked close to tears.

A rotund, grey haired lady with arms like Popeye emerged from the kitchen, wringing her hands on her apron, clearly anxious that the foreigners enjoyed their food.

Eventually, under the interested gaze of everyone in the place, we finished.

"Bloody hell, that was filling," Norman gasped as he wiped his mouth and pushed away his plate.

Gill and I said nothing. We had seen the old lady, now beaming, bringing three more steaming plates from the kitchen.

Good as the food and hospitality was, we never seemed to find the time to return to that particular venue.

As time went by, it became clear that there was much more to be learned about selling that could be obtained from the training courses.

Some days everything would go according to plan and at other times the same formula would fail miserably. This was mainly due to that unpredictable element, the customer.

I was told that our contact at an account in Leicester was mad about dogs and a mention of these creatures would serve to make him receptive. However, when I told this gentleman that I was taking over the area from our agent's representative, he responded with, "Thank goodness, all he ever talked about was bloody dogs!"

Despite the best laid plans of mice and sales strategists, you still had to make most of it up as you went along.

As time went by I began learn how to handle the unexpected problems that prospective customers could throw at you, but still got caught off guard on occasions.

One such time was when I arrived for a meeting with the Shipping Manager of a company in the rag trade in Birmingham.

"Good morning," I said to the pretty girl in the reception cubicle "I have an appointment with Mr. Abrahams".

She smiled sweetly but did not reply. She then removed her dress to reveal a matching bra and panties.

I coughed loudly and again announced the purpose of my visit, but by now she was removing her bra, having discreetly turned her back on me.

At that point I was intercepted by a harridan kitted out like a Breton widow who propelled me towards the front door while berating me for using the reception area while a fashion show was in progress.

Finally, as I was being propelled through the door I was told that Mr Abrahams would not be available until the following day.

"I'm quite prepared to wait," I vainly appealed to the now closing portal.

I also learned that pride comes before a fall. Once, after winning a substantial contract, I was so elated that I accidentally left the building via the window rather than the more conventional door. Not quite as dramatic as it sounds, as the large, full length window was being replaced and it was a simple mistake to step over the low sill and into the garden rather than the car park.

Unfortunately, it had been raining heavily and I sank ankle deep in mud. I thought of stepping back into the reception area, but realised that my muddy footprints across the highly polished marble floor would make my visit even more memorable, so I squelched my way across the garden, feeling hundreds of eyes on me as I sought the refuge of my car.

In the world of sales, triumph and disaster were near neighbours and could often be heavily disguised until the last moment.

On one occasion, I ignored Norman's advice to visit a company who were located next door to our main rivals and to everyone's surprise, came away with the business. It was their very proximity to our competitors that secured our winning the account. The company had noticed our vehicle pass their door at around 4pm every day on its way to a regular collection nearby. This was a time that suited them far better than having to wait until our rival's vehicle arrived back at the end of the day.

On the other side of the coin, I lost an account because an opposition salesman had a heart attack while visiting their office, something I was unwilling to do.

Over all, I think Norman was quite pleased with my progress and was the life and soul of the party when Ellen and I got married in June.

He was certainly leading the celebrations when Ellen and I set off on honeymoon with our Best Man, David Richardson. No, David did not join us on the honeymoon, but Birch Coppice could not spare two players that afternoon and as we headed north for the Lake District we first had to deliver David, who was also our fast bowler, to the appropriate cricket ground.

After a lovely week in Ambleside my first day back at work was a fairly relaxed one. The boys were in a leg pulling mood, Gill was far too inquisitive and even Norman seemed content to give me an easy day. It was only on my way home to my new wife that evening that I received a reminder of how things could suddenly go horribly wrong.

I was overtaken by a motorcyclist just before a sharp bend. As he swept through the corner, his footrest hit the ground, the bike cartwheeled and the rider hit a telegraph pole.

As the only witness, I had to describe the events to the Coroner's court. The questions I had to answer ensured that the rider's parents and fiancee had to suffer every detail.

I have never forgotten that boy's name and can only hope that the passing years have eased the pain that I was unable to spare his loved ones.

Back at work we were starting to make the transition from a Sales Office to a fully operational depot. While I was still employed as a salesman, it was not unusual to find me typing air waybills, labelling freight, sweeping the warehouse, loading lorries and making collections and deliveries.

There was even a permanent memorial on the warehouse wall to the only occasion on which I was permitted to reverse the three-tonner onto the loading bay!

On occasions, I also interviewed job applicants and remember a young school leaver coming for for a job when, whilst our warehouse was complete, our office had not been fitted out and we were working out of an old builder's shed on the canal bank at Acock's Green.

The floor of this hut was encrusted with a residue of concrete, since it had been used to to mix cement. We had stapled maps and photographs over holes in the walls and the lighting was delivered by a cable through the window from a socket in the building next door.

It was in this pioneering environment that I attempted to enthuse the lad with the airfreight industry and paint a romantic picture of the world's largest airfreight company.

As the interview progressed, a torrential downpour of rain commenced and rivulets of water cascaded down the canal bank, past the shed and into the canal. Eventually, after the shed had slithered down the slope two or three times towards the water's edge I thought it time to ask the lad whether he wanted the job, before we had to swim for our lives.

The boy, whose name was Cyril, must have seen beyond the immediate surroundings, for he took the job and several years later became the company's Service Manager at Heathrow.

In due course, the transformation was complete and we had a smart office and warehouse, with trucks, drivers, clerks and even and additional salesman, so my days of driving from Derby to Birmingham on a Friday night with my car so heavily laden with bales of carbon fibre that I could not sit properly in the driving seat were finally over. However, as the carbon fibre was intended for the heat shields on the Apollo spacecraft, I proudly claim it as my contribution to the space race!

So, after eighteen months of struggle and unpredictable hours, Norman found himself promoted to Midlands Area Manager, while I had reached the dizzy heights of Senior Salesman for the Midlands.

My home life had also been subject to a certain amount of change during this hectic period. When Ellen and I got married, we moved into an apartment in Sheepy Magna, near Market Bosworth.

If that sounds rural, it really was. Apart from the occasional bleat or moo, when I switched off the car's engine all was silent. The flat itself was in and old hunting lodge that had once belonged to Admiral Howe, who had commanded the British fleet during the American War of Independence.

It was fairly remote from everywhere but the Bosworth battlefield, which we visited a couple of times, and the Mallory Park motorcycle circuit, where I was a regular, although Ellen only seemed to want to join me when Giacomo Agostini was on the bill.

Set in beautiful grounds, our rambling mansion had been divided into four huge, if somewhat eccentrically laid out, apartments. Ours had a beautiful living room, with a large bay window overlooking the garden, great for parties. The kitchen was similarly spacious, allowing Ellen and I to indulge in the occasional game of indoor cricket.

The decoration was not so impressive and the temptation to poke a finger through the wallpaper where it had rounded off a square corner was almost unbearable.

But we were newly wed and happy - apart from the day when I was off work with a cold and Ellen kindly lit a fire for me in the bedroom. We discovered that the chimney was blocked and for a couple of days the room was better suited to curing kippers than convalescence.

After eighteen months we decided to get on the property ladder and moved into a three bedroom semi-detached house in Belgrave, Tamworth.

It cost us a massive £3,200 and so we were mortgaged up to the hilt, but it was in a pleasant little development, with good neighbours and quite close to an excellent fish and chip shop.

It was also a timely moment for us to put down some roots for soon we were to be expecting an addition to the family. Though preparations were made for a home delivery, including raising the legs of the bed onto bricks, the baby seemed very reluctant to put in an appearance.

Eventually, a couple of weeks after the due date, Ellen was taken into hospital in Sutton Coldfield in case the baby preferred to be born in a more up-market address.

It was there, on a Sunday lunchtime, with hardly any staff on duty, I was issued with a pair of rubber gloves and told to be ready to assist. Then, at the crucial moment, a gaggle of nurses turned up and I was unceremoniously bundled out of the room.

In those days, fathers were not welcome at the birth.

It was sometime after midnight when I finally saw my daughter, but it was well worth the wait. She did not appear to be equally impressed.

I drove home to Tamworth in the early hours of the morning, tired, hungry and the happiest man in the world.

Our new member of the family brought with her many changes to our way of life, but changes were afoot at work as well.

In addition to the development in Birmingham, the company was going through a period of expansion throughout the country, creating opportunities for promotion.

As the oldest of our managers and nearest to

retirement, Norman had ruled himself out of the upheaval and had no wish to leave Birmingham, but he did indicate that I might be in line for an approach.

I thought this unlikely, but one Saturday morning soon afterwards I received a phone call from our U.K. General Manager.

"What do you know about Scotland?" he asked.

North to Scotland

Storm clouds darkened the sky, the wind howled through the telephone wires and the rain lashed past horizontally as we stepped from the local train at Prestwick station to get our first glimpse of the place that would be our home for the next six years.

It could not have made a better effort to deter us and the look on Ellen's face mirrored my own unspoken gloom.

The promised car to meet us was nowhere to be seen and the mention of a taxi only brought a smile to the face of the inhabitant of the ticket office.

After a phone call and about twenty minutes of comparing the dismal weather outside to the equally dreary decor inside, the car finally arrived and whisked us away on the fully two minute drive to the office.

This was our inspection visit to Scotland after Emery's U.K. General Manager had offered me the opportunity to transfer from Birmingham to try to revive the flagging fortunes of the Prestwick and Glasgow offices.

It was January 1970, Ellen and I had been married for three and a half years, our daughter Sarah was six months old and I was a few weeks away from my thirtieth birthday.

Whilst we had been given a few days visit to decide whether we wanted to make the move, it was never really in doubt. Despite the wretched weather on our arrival, it would have taken a tsunami to sweep in off the Clyde and wash away the airport for us to refuse.

Having met the staff, toured the airport and had a brief introduction to the Land o' Burns, it became a matter of finding somewhere to live and, more importantly, to sell our house in Tamworth.

Not that the Birmingham office had quite finished with me. Just before what turned out to be my last Christmas in the Midlands, Norman asked me to take our Service Manager, Norman Neale, to meet our agents in Leicester, since I had been their only point of contact for the last few years.

On our way back to Birmingham, Norman decided he wanted a cup of tea and suggested we stop at Market Bosworth. As I had lived in nearby Sheepy Magna for the first eighteen months of my married life, I thought I knew Bosworth pretty well and suggested that alien abduction was more likely than finding a cafe in that tiny town. But Norman, with all the boldness that had carried him through the Arnhem campaign, told me to turn down a narrow side street and to my surprise we found a small cafe.

The cafe was empty apart from the man behind the counter, who seemed surprised that customers were interrupting his reverie. He rather glumly took our order for two teas and disappeared into the kitchen.

After a while, we noticed the unmistakeable smell of burning. "I don't know how you can burn tea." said Norman. Within a few moments, however, the mystery was solved and we jumped out of our seats when we saw the wallpaper and curtains on fire. Not only that, but the lino and the paint on the skirting board were melting.

On entering the cafe, we had inadvertently knocked over an electric fire, which had rolled onto its grille and come to rest face down at the foot of the wall.

We beat out the flames, set the fire upright and turned to see the owner standing aghast, a cup of tea in each hand. "You've set fire to my cafe," he said, rather superfluously.
"I think you'll find we saved it", replied Norman. "We put the fire out."
"All for two bloody cups of tea!" said the disgruntled caterer.

On my last working day in Birmingham, I attempted to take our new trainee salesman,

Don, on some joint sales calls. I had just told him of how my own first call was scuppered by a puncture when, without warning, the car windscreen shattered.

Something was telling me it was time to go!

At the time of our move to Scotland, it just so happened that Tamworth was undergoing a sizeable expansion, with with the view of housing thousands of Birmingham's surplus inhabitants. But as is so often the case, the planners and plannees did not see things from the same viewpoint, with many of the intended immigrants refusing to move, while others who did, having been made warmly unwelcome by the indigenous population, returned home as soon as the opportunity presented itself.

As a result, at the time we were trying to sell our three bedroom semi, there were hundreds more, some never occupied, on the market.

So for six long months I was staying in "digs" during the week and setting off on Friday evenings or Saturday lunchtimes to get home to see my family, while Ellen was desperately trying to sell our house and bring up baby Sarah.

My temporary accommodation in Prestwick could not have been better. The elderly couple who ran the B&B were lovely people.

In fact, in order to get away promptly after work on Friday evenings, I was forced to sneak out unseen, for if the lady of the house caught me she would not permit me to set out on such a long journey without a good meal.

In those days before the motorway was completed, it was a six to six and a half hour journey, to be repeated after lunch on Sunday in the opposite direction.

During my solo stint at Prestwick, I worked late and usually ate out and on one evening I went into a Chinese restaurant in Ayr to find it being run by the chap who had operated our local takeaway in Tamworth. He had moved at the same time as me. I did not realise that I had been such a good a customer!

I also got involved in the regular Tuesday night domino school at the Steamboat pub on Ayr docks, the only time in my life I have been a "regular" at any local hostelry.

I did not expect to see a reminder of home on Ayr docks, so it was quite a surprise that the first lorry I saw there belonged to the Elford bowler who had sportingly, if unsuccessfully, lobbed up a friendly delivery in an attempt to give me my first century at Birch Coppice eleven years earlier!

At first I went home every second weekend,

so I became familiar with Kilmarnock and Ayr United football grounds, but as the months passed and the pressure began to tell on us I went home every weekend, even when I had to go to work on the Saturday morning.

On one of my first weekends in Scotland, I decided to try to find a long lost cousin I had never met, the daughter of one of my mother's sisters with whom contact had been lost after the family schism.

Finding her involved taking the ferry from Gourock to Dunoon. On a subsequent crossing with Ellen, we had the startling sight of a nuclear submarine surfacing in our wake, but on this occasion the views of the loch were sufficiently enchanting without military intervention.

After driving up the hill out of Dunoon, I found the cottage and knocked. The door opened a fraction and a wizened, elderly man's face appeared. I guessed this was my cousin Peggy's husband, Norman, and explained who I was. He muttered something I could not understand and closed the door. Within seconds it reopened and I was confronted by a woman who looked remarkably like my mother. Within moments I found myself sitting in front of a plate of roast beef and all the trimmings, produced as if by magic. Clearly, the family feud was over.

On another memorable occasion, I attended a motorcycle race meeting on the beach at Prestwick and realised that a few random moments of pleasure did not constitute a way of life and could not continue.

I phoned my boss and told him that if the company would not relieve us of the problem of selling our house I would have to resign.

It was fortunate that things were going well at work, for if my bluff had been called I do not know what I would have done.

Needless to say, no sooner had I persuaded the company to take the house of our hands than Ellen found a buyer.

Shortly before Ellen and Sarah joined me in Scotland, a bizarre incident happened following my appearance at Hamilton Sheriff's Court, after I had assisted the police at the scene of an accident.

Although I had told the police that I was working out of Prestwick, my home address was still Tamworth and I was, therefore to receive my travelling expenses for the whole round trip.
So it came as a shock to Ellen when, late on a Friday night a policeman knocked on our door. She knew I would be making my way

over the Shap and down to the Midlands via the M6 and feared that I had been involved in an accident.

In fact, in the strange way the police had of settling their debts, the officer had merely arrived to pay my travelling expenses!

With our house in Tamworth now sold, I was now looking in earnest for somewhere to live in Ayrshire. I had been looking around for some time and had my name on various lists, but the few places I had been offered were quite strange - weird little flats above shops and a poky crofter's cottage. But now, just as it was needed most, I found something habitable, although it was by no means less odd than some of the other places I had seen.

It was a first floor flat in the grounds of a country estate called Fairlie House at Gatehead, about a fifteen minute drive from my office at the airport. Sounds nice?

It was called Garage Cottage. That is to say, it was a garage pretending to be a cottage, with the accommodation being located in the roof above the vehicle garaging area. The kitchen had to be worn rather than entered, while the cat had to get used to being put out at night onto the roof from where it seemed to be able to make its way down to the ground.

Any garaged vehicles could be seen through the holes in the bathroom floor. Heaven only knows what any people below could see! Fortunately the garage was seldom used so we never found out.

So, at long last, Ellen, Sarah, our cat, furniture and personal impedimenta made the journey northwards.
By now, I had got to know and like my staff in Scotland and they enthusiastically offered to do the removals for us. We borrowed one of the Prestwick trucks and spent a last night encamped in Tamworth before setting off, the three tonner in the lead, with Ellen's prized rubber plant lashed outside the cab because it was too tall to travel inside. (It also turned out to be too tall for our flat and spent a couple of years in my office before finally outgrowing that and being presented to the airport's passenger terminal, which had a ceiling high enough to cope with it's ambitions.)

My father had recently retired, so he and my mother decided to join the migration, partly to help us move and partly for a holiday.

Ellen, Sarah and I set off last, after a final tidy-up. The plan was that all three vehicles would meet up at a designated service area on the motorway, but this did not happen and we never saw any of our group all the way to Prestwick.

Had mobile phones been invented, we could have kept in contact, but as it was we just had to press on and hope all was well with the rest of the party.

The lorry, its occupants desperate to arrive first, swept on without a stop and were unloaded by the time we rolled up.

Sadly, we did not avoid the fun of getting our furniture up the narrow staircase, but after several breaks for hysterical laughter, all was eventually in place and the move completed.

The only one not satisfied with the outcome was the cat. He quickly decided that he did not enjoy being pursued through the undergrowth by the estate dogs and a month or so after we arrived he went to live with the rabbits in a nearby field. We saw him from time to time and he even occasionally acknowledged our greeting, but he was certainly no longer a house cat.

When we moved in were quite surprised to find the telephone was connected, so I phoned the GPO to let them know that we wished to take over the rental from that date. The Post Office clearly got the message, for a few days later we received a bill for over four hundred pounds and were promptly disconnected!

It did not help that the lady on their

complaints desk had such a bad speech impediment it was difficult for me to give full vent to my anger and it took about a week for us to be reconnected without penalty.

We were only at Gatehead for six months but in that time much happened. Sarah learned to walk and to much rejoicing finally made it all the way down the long corridor to her bedroom in one attempt.

Towards the end of my parents' visit, Dad and I went up to Greenock to see Morton play West Bromwich Albion. I think it must have been in the old Anglo-Scottish Cup competition. It was there that I noticed my father was more than a bit under the weather and suggested he see the doctor for a check-up when he got home.

The first football match my father took me to see when I was a little boy involved West Brom and it turned out that they also took part in the last one I took him to see, although neither of us were "Baggies" supporters.

The doctor gave my father six months and proved to be a good judge. We were preparing to evacuate Garage Cottage when we got the news of his death. I had only just returned from the Midlands and had been with him earlier in the day. He had drifted between the past and present, with a complete grasp of the surprising defeat of Leeds United by Colchester in their F.A. Cup tie on the previous day, but then explaining why the handbrake is required to be on the outside of a car, which must have been some long forgotten regulation.

Shortly after dad's funeral, Mr Lyon, the husband of my former landlady in Prestwick, also died and another lovely man was lost to us.

With the end of our six month tenure in sight, we were struggling to find a more permanent home and were beginning to feel anxious when we were contacted out of the blue by an organisation called the Scottish Special Housing Association, one of the many groups I had contacted when first moving north of the border.

They phoned early one morning as I was getting ready for work and said they had a house for us just a few miles away in Symington and would we like to take a look?

We went immediately and found it was actually closer to my office than Gatehead. It was a new house, not quite ready for occupation, but waiting only for the finishing touches like telephone connection. It was in a square of houses surrounding a common village green. There was also a garage in an adjacent parking area.

The rent was £25 per month and as we seemed quite sure we wanted it, we might as well have the keys straight away!

The deal was done in a matter of minutes and the SSHA representative then staggered off, minus the keys, nursing a badly shaken hand.

After so much gloom, something really good had happened.

One remarkable social event took place during our short stay at Gatehead - our first New year in Scotland. All the staff were invited round and Ellen had prepared a variety of delicacies and stocked the drinks cabinet.

As ten o'clock passed we wondered why no one had put in an appearance and after the chimes of midnight we wished each other a Happy New Year and decided they must have all found better parties.

It was about half past midnight when the first knock came on the door, just as we were thinking of calling it a day.

We had been totally unaware that the local tradition demanded that you only set out to a New Year's party after midnight had struck.

Soon the flat was crowded and both food and drink disappearing rapidly, despite the generous reinforcements brought by our guests.

One of our drivers, Big Alex, mixed grape and grain, which had the effect of turning his bones to rubber and when, around four a.m. the party started to wind down, the problem of getting the giant highlander down our narrow staircase could be postponed no longer.

He could, of course, have slept guiltlessly on our floor, but Alex was not a man to be easily swayed. In fact, swaying was the one thing of which he seemed perfectly capable without any assistance. With several of us supporting his weight, we managed to get him downstairs, though his feet seemed more inclined to walk down the wall instead of the stairs.

Finally out into the fresh morning air, we faced the problem of dissuading him from driving himself home. Alistair, one of our other drivers, told me that no one was brave enough to tell Alex he was in no condition to drive.
Gifted with a sudden brainwave, I said, "Goodness me, Alex, a Ford Classic! I've always wanted to drive one of these." The genial giant held open the door, bowed solemnly and handed me the keys.

As Gilbert, our Senior Service Agent was,

like me, a lightweight when it came to drinking, I asked him to follow us at a discreet distance, so that I could make a rapid getaway when I had deposited Alex at his parents' house.

Alex's father was the gravedigger and caretaker at cemetery at Shewelton and lived in a cottage in the centre of the graveyard. After driving carefully through the pre-dawn fog with my now vocal passenger, we finally arrived at the iron gated cemetery. I went to open the gates but on my return discovered that my inebriated companion had already disembarked. I called his name, then walked up to the front door and knocked, to no avail. Finally, I went back out of the gates to be sure he was not lying in the road. He was nowhere to be seen. Neither, for that matter, was Gilbert.

Finding yourself in a foggy graveyard, in your shirtsleeves, at four-thirty on New Year's morning is a sobering experience in itself and I now also seemed to be facing a walk of several miles home.

Fortunately I had only reached the end of the cemetery wall when I came upon Gilbert's car, parked without lights and containing a noticeably shaken Gilbert.

He had followed us and reached the cemetery gates as I must have been parking Alex's car at the cottage. Peering into the now silent cemetery, he had called out, "Halloo, Alan,"

No reply. He called again and this time a foggy giant loomed up from behind a gravestone. "Wha's at?" roared the misty apparition, whereupon Gilbert, never a man to challenge the supernatural, fled to the safety of his car.

We assume the scary leviathan must have been Alex, but we never asked him.

Just in case it wasn't.

Life beyond the Wall

We quickly got to like Prestwick. Despite its forbidding red sandstone and "wee windaes", it was never as gloomy as it appeared on our first visit. In addition to its charming seafront, with views of Arran, it was pleasantly equipped with refined tearooms, fine bakeries, restaurants and, eventually, a supermarket.

It also had a cricket club, but more of that later.

Sheltered by the hills and warmed by the North Atlantic Drift, it escaped the worst of the weather and in our six years there, we only saw one morning's snow and even that was gone by mid afternoon. Yet only a few miles inland deep snow could often cause traffic problems and I once slithered across the Glenifer Braes to Paisley only to be met by the police at the foot of the hills, apologising for not being able to prevent me from using a road that had just been closed.

The airport was a very sociable place and inter company rivalries were often set aside for extra-mural activities. The airport club arranged a number of outings to places of interest, like the Hunterston nuclear power station, where even the luminous dial on a wristwatch would be picked up by the geiger counters on hand to monitor radioactivity.

Another trip was made to Killock Colliery, one of the deepest mines in the country, where the miners amused themselves by frightening the lives out of us, firing a "shot" without warning us in advance. The sudden flash of light in the darkness, followed by the rush of air, smell of cordite and the roar of the explosion convinced many of our party that we had been involved in an accident, while one of our number conceded that, as far as he was concerned, he had!

We also visited the Royal Navy base on the far side of the airport, where we were shown over a Sea King search and rescue helicopter. After various pieces of sophisticated equipment had been explained to us, we were asked if there were any questions. "Yes," said a little voice from the back. "Where is the ladies toilet?"

The main event in the Airport Club's social calendar was the Treasure Hunt, which involved carloads of competitors following clues to find a pub where a meal had been arranged and answering a number of silly questions about things seen along the route.

On one occasion the sentry outside the U.S. Navy base got so fed up with being asked how many stripes there were on the U.S. flag that as soon as our car pulled up he said, "Thirteen, goddamit!"

Another year, we got so lost that darkness fell and in trying to read a clue by the light of a match, the clue sheet caught fire, so that was the end of that night's adventure. Claims that Gilbert deliberately burned the sheet to prevent further aimless wandering around the west of Scotland were never satisfactorily dispelled, but whatever the truth, we were forced to phone rally control to retire from the competition and be told of the venue for dinner.

To avoid similar embarrassment in future, Team Emery nobly volunteered to run the treasure hunt in future years which proved to be far more fun than taking part.

Our move from Gatehead to Symington was also performed by the gang from work, this time under the guidance of our Service Supervisor, Jimmy. His advice on furniture removal consisted of standing back and saying, "Tilt it. Tilt it." So often would he give this detailed instruction that for several months after, any problem at work was likely to dealt with by someone suggesting, "Tilt it!"

I was very fortunate in the team I inherited at Prestwick and Glasgow, including the member of staff that my predecessor recommended I should fire as my first action in taking over.

I rather felt that if the guy was not bad enough to fire as the leaving manager's last act, he was good enough for me to at least give him the opportunity to establish his worth. As it turned out, he and the others took advantage of the fresh start and immediately began to tackle the problems that had placed the future of the Scottish offices in question.

That is not to say they were not an unusual bunch of characters.

Of all the words to describe my second in command, Jimmy, "modest" would not appear in the first two volumes. Had he been as accomplished a footballer, rugby player, athlete or golfer as his many stories of his youth implied, we would all have heard of him. Had he been as good a gambler as he claimed, we would all have been working for him.

He would often tell me how much he had won on the horses, but always omitted to mention how much he had lost between winnings.

I once saw him win a £50 jackpot on a fruit machine, only then to watch him feed it all back in during the course of the evening.

One thing he did not brag about was his knowledge of the air freight business. He did not need to boast about that.

The only problem I had with him at the outset was that my appointment came as a major disappointment to him. Though I did not learn of it until later, the company had given him a free trip to Hong Kong so that he would be well out of the way when I visited Prestwick to discuss the appointment that he was expecting to receive.

Under those circumstances it is hardly surprising that he had a bit of a chip on his shoulder when I arrived on the scene.

Eventually we became good allies and the only problem I had with him was that he used to tell his wife that I had him working late when he was actually at the Steamboat Inn or the bookies!

I finally discovered why his wife seemed a little frosty towards me when Ellen and I met her in the supermarket a few minutes after he had phoned her to say he would be late as I had called him in to a meeting at the office!

Jimmy was also involved in the first serious incident I had to deal with during my early months in Scotland.

Not famed for his tact and diplomacy, he had managed to upset Big Alex to the point that Alex had picked up the wee man and thrown him across the Abbotsinch office. I arrived a few minutes after the incident, just as Alex drove away to make the late collection that had been the subject of their discussion.

I found Jimmy, clearly shaken and for once almost speechless. The niceties of who started the disagreement and who said what were irrelevant, since physical violence was an automatic dismissal offence.

Accordingly, I summoned Alex to my office the following morning. I was more than a little apprehensive, as I had never fired anyone before, let alone a giant highlander with a known short fuse.

I need not have worried, for the contrite driver immediately told me he knew I had no choice but to sack him and apologised for letting me down! He also added somewhat darkly that he would almost certainly do the same again had I given him the chance.

My secretary, Muriel, had spent some years as a children's nanny in America, smoked like a chimney, swore like a trooper and was refreshingly direct.

She was a reluctant spinster, a status not helped by the fact that life seemed to hold little romance in her eyes, particularly in view of the vigour with which she beat off the attentions of a member of staff who had unfortunately made her the object of his desires.

As she often stayed overnight with friends or went out directly from work, she always arrived in the mornings laden with enough luggage to see her through until she next made it home.

This impedimenta sometimes included her dog, an unpleasant little Jack Russell whose bark was only worse than its bite in that it barked even more frequently that it bit.

As it would let out a stream of vitriol every time the phone rang, it became a popular game, whenever Muriel was out of the office rearranging her makeup, to alternately ring all the telephone extensions and watch with evil satisfaction as the poisonous little dwarf exhausted itself running from one phone to the next.

Eventually, it bit me once too often and was condemned to to spend its day staring hatefully at me from its position of vantage in the car park.

I am happy to relate that Muriel eventually found Mr Right to take on the responsibility for her and her hell-hound.
Davy, our salesman, was a really pleasant lad who loved sea fishing and, judging by the fish he sometimes brought in for me on a

Monday morning, was very good at it.

Unfortunately, though he seldom had to resort to fisherman's tales, his salesman's tales were legendary. Davy could come up with more excuses for not making a sales call than I have heard from all the other salesmen I have ever worked with.

He could go for a whole week without actually coming face to face with a prospective customer. Other times he would disappear for days without us being able to track him down.

I tried to motivate him, encourage him, take him on joint calls, set him reward targets, tell him off and threaten him but nothing worked.

My frustration peaked to overflowing when his company car came up for replacement. Our vehicle supplier was based in Kent, hardly convenient for Scotland, so as I was due to attend a meeting in Manchester, I asked one of our London boys to drive the new car up to the meeting and I would drive Davy's car down so we could make the change over with the least inconvenience.

Davy, who normally operated in the east of Scotland, breezed into Prestwick on the appointed day with a cheery, "All fuelled up, boss!"

Only then did I see that all four tyres were completely bald, with no vestige of tread. There was no way I was going to let the car go all the way to London in that condition.

I knew I would get a rocket for buying a new set of tyres on the last day of the contract, but that was nothing to the ICBM I would receive if I risked it and the car was involved in some mishap on the way south.

As there was a tyre replacement company a couple of miles away on the bypass, I decided to call in there and hope for a quick fix. When I got there I found to my horror that there were three police cars, one being driven into the service bay and two others waiting their turn. I parked as far from them as I could and wondered how long I would have to wait before I could be on my way to Manchester.

My anxiety did not diminish when I saw Big Alex, our ex-driver, striding towards me from the office. I had no idea he had got a job there. Once again, the giant highlander came to my rescue.

"Get that vehicle out of there," he bellowed to the policeman who had just driven into the service bay. "I've got a cash customer here. You lot can wait."

Fortunately, the police acquiesced, showed

no interest in me or my bald tyres and I was on my way rejoicing in a very short time.

I struggled on for another month or so with Davy's lack of productivity before persuading him that he really did not want to be an airfreight salesman and should try something else.

I was sorry to lose him, as he was a likeable character, as well as a supplier of fine fish, but we had not seen the last of him.

He got a job with Dexion, a company which fitted out warehouses, and he often popped in to see us with details of airfreight shipments he had seen in the warehouses he was measuring up. It is quite strange to say that we got far more useful input from him after he had left us than ever we did while he was on our payroll.

Our office junior, Andrew, was a keen young lad who it was impossible to dislike and who shared my support for Ayr Bruins Ice Hockey team. His main shortcoming was his ability to misinterpret almost every instruction given to him and to take almost everything said to him in a completely literal sense. While this often made him a target for jokes from the other lads, even I could not defend him when, as an aspiring high jumper, he complained about being beaten by a one-legged opponent, claiming that his nemesis had the unfair advantage of only having to get one leg over the bar!

But my fondest memory of Andy was the morning he burst into my office in a state of agitation and announced, "Mr. Brown, we have an import shipment that I think you will have to phone the consignee yourself." When I asked him to explain, he told me, "It's for Paul McCartney!"
When I asked him who was on imports that morning, Andy admitted that it was himself. "Then you phone him," I replied.

Later in the day, a relaxed and confident Andy popped his head round the door. "Oh, by the way," he said, "Paul was'nae home, so I had a chat with Linda and everything is under control!"

When, after a couple of years, Andy left us to become a roadie with a pop group, we missed his cheery manner and his willingness to go to the canteen for cheese and mushroom rolls, but felt he had probably made the right choice.

These were the people, with Gilbert, Iain, Alistair and Knox, who formed my team in our early days in Scotland.

Oil on Troubled Waters

When I took on the responsibility for Emery's Scottish offices, my predecessor told me that I must take great care of the two major customers, IBM and the U.S. Navy, for if we lost those we would be unable to continue our operations north of the border.

Needless to say, in time we lost them both, though through no fault of our own. Both losses involved their import shipments, with IBM in Greenford, Middlesex, deciding to piggyback their Scottish requirements onto charter flights into London and the U.S. Navy being obliged to cede their control to the U.S. Military Airlift flights into Mildenhall.

This left us with IBM's export shipments, which were sufficiently frequent for us to phone them each morning at 10.00am to establish their requirements for the day.

On one notable occasion our ten o'clock call resulted in our being told that there was no freight that day. About half an hour later they called us back to tell us they had 38 tons for Toronto on its way down to us from Greenock.

In those days, before the advent of the wide bodied "Jumbos", that amount was just about an entire freighter load. It took up all the space available on all four BOAC and Air

Canada cargo and passenger flights and we even needed to persuade Air Canada to divert their London to Toronto freighter into Prestwick, but we got the whole load away that night.

It was fortunate that by the time we lost our two major customers we had added so many smaller accounts that it not only made up the shortfall, but made us less dependent on any single source of business.

Building up the business was usually just a hard slog, but this makes boring reading and it is more interesting to focus on a few exceptions.

Emery's Sales Manual told me I should never wait for more than twenty minutes to see a prospective customer, so I was just about to leave the reception area of an engineering company in Cathcart when my contact came running down the stairs. He apologised for keeping me waiting and said he had been on the phone to a supplier in the U.S.A. trying to trace an airfreight shipment.
"That's a shame," I replied, "If we had been carrying it your call would not have been necessary."
That was my entire sales pitch. "Give me two minutes", he said and ran back upstairs. He returned with about a dozen U.S. company details. "What do I need to do?" he asked.

He did not want to know how we would provide the service he needed nor, to the best of my knowledge, did he ever ask us to trace a shipment. He just became a satisfied customer.

Another occasion was even easier. I phoned a company in Port Glasgow for an appointment, introduced myself and was asked, "Are you from Tamworth?" The Scottish voice on the other end of the phone even used the Midlands pronunciation of "Tamuth". My confirmation was the only qualification I appeared to need to get his business!

Being English was not always an advantage, however. Having made several unsuccessful visits to a world famous British company with a plant in Glasgow, I chanced to bump into its Shipping Manager in the terminal building at Glasgow Airport and was surprised when he invited me to join him for a drink while he waited for his flight to be called.

Seated behind his single malt, my contact said, "You know, I thought Emery were mad to send an Englishman to Glasgow. I gave you six months at best, but you are doing O.K. Phone my secretary next week to set up a meeting."

I nearly choked on my orange juice and lemonade. How he could judge if I was doing well or not when he didn't give us any traffic was beyond me, but he was as good as his word and the only topic of our subsequent meeting was which segment of his substantial business we would get.

Another result that was hard earned involved a large American computer company in Fife. It was one of those very frustrating situations where I knew I could not only give a better service than they were getting, but also save them money. But I could not prise my contact off the fence. On one occasion I had told him that if I could just walk him through our transhipment department in New York he would see the benefit for himself.

A few weeks later, I received a phone call from my contact to tell me that his father had just had a major operation and he was going home to New Jersey for a week to be with his dad, but he would find time to visit our New York facility if I would meet him there.

So it was that I took a midday flight to New York, had lunch with a couple of colleagues, met my contact for the promised tour, sealed the deal and flew home the same evening. All in a day's work!

It would be dishonest of me to claim the credit for the resurgence in Emery's fortunes in Scotland and ignore the huge boost provided by the emergence of the North Sea oil industry.

Where once quiet flowed the Don and the Dee, the old Granite City had sprung to life as the land base for the offshore activities.

We plunged into this business with a vengeance, for having offices in the U.S. cities where most of the exploration and drilling companies were based gave us a continuous link between shipper and consignee.

In fact, my first publication, aimed at the American market and completely devoid of poetry, was entitled "The fastest way the the North Sea".

The offshore oil industry was completely crazy, even by the standards of the airfreight business. It was not unknown to get a phone call at 3am, not for some dire emergency, but to query an invoice!

I once tried to check into my hotel in Aberdeen to find the floor in front of the reception desk was occupied by a large, snoring American, clearly sleeping off the effects of the local brew.
"Shouldn't you move him?" I asked the desk clerk.
"For what he pays us, he sleeps where he likes", was the reply.

With the departure of Davy, Jimmy had spent part of his time on Sales in the area local to our offices, but with the growth of the business we hired another salesman, Tom, to cover Edinburgh and the east, while he and I shared the need for greater coverage in the Aberdeen area.

To increase our overall knowledge of the whole process, one of our Houston salesmen, Tommy Walker, visited Scotland, while Tom and I both visited Houston, Dallas and New Orleans.

It was interesting to note the different approach to Sales in America. The Dallas salesmen arrived at the office at around 7.30am and had a pep talk from the Sales Manager before driving off in different directions, only to meet up at a diner a couple of miles down the road for breakfast!

The Houston team were a little more realistic and I liked their keenness to learn about the Scottish end of our operation. In fact, without the prompting of their manager, they took me to dinner one evening and questioned me about our handling from Prestwick to ultimate destination until they were happy for me to question them on it. I think this was the idea of one of the sales team, Richard Pinger, who later left the company to become an attorney.

New Orleans was much more laid back. I was particularly pleased when our manager dropped me off at my hotel on my first night in town and said, "We got an early start in the morning, Al. I'll pick you up around ten."

The trip to the wild west was a great success, but not without incident. At an Offshore Exhibition we had been giving away imitation banknotes as an advertising gimmick and it was to the amusement of my American colleagues that I was accosted in the street by an exotic dancer who had received a number of these banknotes placed in various recesses of her anatomy only to discover they were fake. She accused me of spreading counterfeit money around Texas and of costing her $5,000. Whilst I suppose the first charge was technically correct, I felt obliged to point out that the money was Confederate and not legal even if it had been genuine. As for the $5,000, I had to tell her that I could not imagine her benefactors would have been quite so generous if the banknotes had been real. Fortunately, the young lady was then bundled away, for I think if we had come to blows I may well have come off worst.

Another potentially lethal situation arose on my very last day in Houston. The sales team had decided that my final experience of Texas would be a holiday and one of their number, a genial giant called Bill Gasch, who reminded me of Hoss Cartwright from the "Bonanza" TV series, took me on a sightseeing trip. Among the places we visited were the San Jacinto battlefield, where Texas won its independence from Mexico, and the First World War battleship "Texas".

Our journey included a drive across a causeway, but Bill had got his timings wrong and the water was soon lapping around the car and dry land slowly disappearing from sight.

It would be an understatement to say that I was becoming apprehensive, but poor Bill was really getting scared. "What's the boss gonna say? I've drowned our guest and lost a company car!" At least he had accepted his own imminent demise as an acceptable loss.

Eventually, the water began to recede, the road reappeared and our journey continued as far as the nearest hostelry.

So my trip to Texas finished with spirits undampened, even if the same could not be said for the car's brake pads.

I really got to like the Houston team and their boss, Charlie Jones, who I later had the pleasure of entertaining back in Scotland .

The six years I spent in Scotland saw the Aberdeen and Dundee area turn from a backwater to a powerhouse, growing faster than its infrastructure.

The first time I saw Aberdeen airport it tiny terminal building with, I think, just a single departure gate. But it rapidly became the busiest helicopter airport in the world.

I also remember going to Dundee's Riverside Airport to meet a small charter aircraft bringing in some urgent replacement parts. I was unfamiliar with the airport but found the terminal building in good time and met the duty manager. He appeared to be the only person there and we got chatting as we awaited the flight.

Eventually he received a phone call and then told me that I would have to leave the building. I asked for the reason and was told that it was for security purposes. "Your aircraft is about to arrive and I have to lock the building while I am out lighting the runway!" he added.

I had a mental picture of him lighting lanterns along the edge of the landing strip, but it was not quite as bad as that.

It was an unpredictable few years north of the border. But all in all it was great fun and it helped the man with his name on the side of our trucks to get richer.

At least I hope it made him much wealthier,

Scotsport

If "Scotsport" seems an odd chapter title, it is a nod in the direction of one of Emery's drivers, Peter McIlvenny, whose wife worked on what was at that time the longest running TV sports programme in the world.

If I have given the impression that my life in Scotland was one of endless work, or that Ellen and Sarah merely basked in the background, my apologies for misleading you.

It is true that for the first few months I did find it heavy going and my loves of cricket, motorcycle racing and poetry were put on hold, but I was comforted in having my family as a good reason for the effort.

Ellen had always contributed on the work front. When we lived in Tamworth she had worked at the industrial branch of Royal Doulton and at the Birmingham Central Library. Even in darkest Leicestershire she had managed to find a job with a sort of international mail order recruitment company in Sheepy Parva, which really was as small as it sounds.

Sarah, for her part, had not only learned to walk, but after we had moved home again into the town of Prestwick, started school and was very quickly at one with her Ayrshire classmates, proudly informing us, "I'm Scots, you're no!"

Ellen took her driving test and resumed her own working career, as Christmas cover at her spiritual home, Marks and Spencer in Ayr and at a furniture store in Prestwick.

It was there that she was able to reintroduce me to cricket, as the husband of one of her work colleagues played for the town team and I was invited to go to a training session.

It proved to be a rapid transformation, as I attended a practice net on a Monday evening and turned out for the first XI in a cup tie at Motherwell two days later.

Prestwick were a great bunch of lads, The skipper, Big John Leven, red haired fast bowler, Alan Appleby, Alan "Twiggy" Dunlop, who I knew from the Clydesdale Bank at the airport, John Duncan, the R.A.F. officer with whom I would open the innings on many occasions and, of course the Scottish sporting legend that was Johnny Hubbard, the South African who had been Rangers' ace penalty taker for many seasons and virtually ran Prestwick's sporting calendar. He organised "Old Firm" Celtic v Rangers Old Boys charity matches, was a tennis coach, played cricket for the town and even masterminded Prestwick's triumphant "It's a Knockout" team.

The club was run under the avuncular eye of its President, Henry Thow, who went on to become President of the Scottish Cricket Union and after whom the Prestwick Oval was later named. It was Henry who turned up at my house one New Year's Day morning to replace a toughened glass front door panel which had proved not tough enough to survive Hogmanay. He refused any payment, even for the materials. "Just keep scoring runs, son", was his only comment.

While the standard of cricket in Scotland was good, with its scattering of overseas Test players, it required a fair amount of travel. Prestwick ranged as far afield as Dumfries in the south and Stirling in the north. A few years after I left and the club gained entry to the new Scottish Premiership, a round trip of nearly four hundred miles to Aberdeen was involved!

I had the usual highs and lows during my five seasons in Scotland and of course it is the highs I remember best.

Getting into the nervous nineties and being last man out in a team total of only 150 stands out. This came in a match at Clarkston on a quagmire of a pitch where the only two boundaries in the match were sixes. The match should never have been played, but as a spell of wet weather had washed out the previous three weekends both teams were desperate to get a game.

I have also bored everyone with the time I opened the innings in a cup semi final against a Kilmarnock side that included the Aussie Bob Massie, who one year later would take 16 England wickets in the Lords Test Match.

My instruction was to see Massie out of the attack so the real batsmen could then score some runs. I was so delighted to see him take his sweater at the end of his spell that I immediately holed out on the boundary to his far less talented replacement.

Still, I suppose I shouldn't complain. That is how I got my wickets for Crowthorne and Wokingham some years later.

Another match I recall was an April season-opener on a bitterly cold afternoon. Our wicket keeper, Tommy Doolan, was injured early in the match and as a specialist slip fielder, I was asked to stand in behind the stumps. Although unused to the position, apart from dropping a few catches and allowing a rather large number of byes, I had a reasonably good match. The only problem was that due to the cold weather my back became so stiff that for two or three days afterwards I could only walk downstairs backwards!

But the most memorable moment in my

playing days in Scotland came with the last league match of the 1972 season, when victory would bring us the championship for the first time, after being runners-up on six previous occasions.

Our visitors, Motherwell, needed a win to secure their safety from relegation and brought a coach load of supporters to cheer them on. But the match itself was an anti-climax, with my own contribution minimal. Although I took the catch that ended Motherwell's innings for less than one hundred runs, I then sat out our own innings waiting to bat at number three, while John Duncan and our new import from Yorkshire, Laurie Bankhead, steered us comfortably to the title.

The party that followed may have started before the tea break but went on into the small hours. At some point, unbeknown to Ellen and I, Johnny Hubbard and John Leven persuaded our daughter Sarah to take her little shopping basket around the assembled merrymakers and tell them that an empty basket needs filling.

By the time Ellen told me it was time we took Sarah home to bed, the basket was so full of money the toddler could hardly lift it, so I had to volunteer to look after it for her.

Having had, by the standards of the rest of

the team, an early night, I wandered down to the clubhouse around 11a.m. the following morning to find about half a dozen bodies still sprawled in guiltless slumber, some of them outside in the yard!

We won the championship a couple more times during my stay at Prestwick, but there was nothing to compare with that first time and being presented with my Prestwick Baggy Blue Bonnet by former Scotland captain, Jimmy Brown.

Whilst I could get my football fix at Kilmarnock and Ayr United, my other passion of motorcycle road racing was ill served in Scotland at that time. I did attend a meeting at Beveridge Park, Kirkcaldy, but while the circuit was picturesque and no doubt very demanding, the slow lap speeds and wise restriction of four riders per race robbed it of the spectacle expected of road racing and I only went on that one occasion.

So when I heard that the Melville Motor Club was experimenting with a disused airfield inside a farm at East Fortune, I got in touch and soon found myself an assistant timekeeper.

There had initially been some concern that the cattle on the infield of the circuit would be distressed by the noise, but this fear proved unfounded, as the cows became keen spectators. They crowded as close to the fence as possible, craning their necks and turning their heads to watch the action, just like their human counterparts.

The facilities for spectators, competitors and officials were temporary and mobile, with the race commentators, lap scorers and timekeepers housed in the upper level of an old double decker bus positioned at the start line. It was certainly primitive, but it brought good quality racing back to Scotland and over the years entertained such T.T. winners as Joey Dunlop, Mick Grant and Alex George.

As the race meetings were held on about four Sundays during the season, my Saturday cricketing commitments were not compromised, though it did call for a ridiculously early start on race day mornings to get to the circuit around 7 a.m.

A few years later, when I had graduated to become chief timekeeper, a specially designed modern circuit was constructed just north of the Forth Bridge and the Melville club was asked to run the opening meeting.

So it was that, double decker and all, we crossed the Forth into Fife and brought racing to Knockhill, which has now developed into a major venue, hosting rounds of the British Superbike Championship. So, finally, shortly before our departure, I had made some tiny contribution to sport in Scotland.

One False Move

Late one evening I wandered through Prestwick's almost deserted terminal building, marvelling at what a great concert hall it would have made, as the canned music reverberated like a symphony orchestra.

On the ground floor, the airline check-in desks were closed, while the airport shop and bank were about to follow suit. Upstairs, the restaurant and bar were about to oust their few lingering customers and silence would soon reign.

I was in the shop buying some sweeties for Sarah when I noticed a dignified inebriate meandering sedately to the counter of the Clydesdale Bank, where my cricketing chum "Twiggy" Dunlop and his colleague "Chick" Robb were on the graveyard shift.

I watched with amusement as the drunk tried to convince Twiggy to accept the pint of beer he was offering to bestow upon him. Twiggy, aware that being seen on duty with a pint of beer would not enhance the bank's sober image, tried to refuse, but his new best friend would not take no for an answer and eventually the embarrassed teller accepted the gift and secreted it under the counter. Honour satisfied, his benefactor went upon his way.

I was about to make my own exit when an American came down the stairs from the restaurant, strode up to Chick's counter and asked to change some traveller's cheques.

It was an opportunity too good to miss. I walked up to Twiggy's adjacent station and said, "Pint of beer, please Twiggy, and put it on my tab." My pal picked up on the gag and solemnly produced the pint of beer. I raised my glass to our transatlantic guest, said "Cheers!" and drank the beer, safe in the knowledge that to this day some corner of the USA believes that Scottish banks sell booze.

Illustrated by such incidents, our years in Scotland sped by, living by turns in Gatehead, Symington and finally in Auchincruive Avenue in Prestwick, which was close enough to my office for me to occasionally make it home for lunch.

The teams I had in place at Prestwick and Glasgow airports had increased our reputation and our business (we even made the lead article in "Scotland" magazine on one occasion). In the time-honoured fashion for Emery, it was the manager who was given all the credit for their success and as a result a number offers of promotion came my way.

Amongst these were the posts of Area Manager for Manchester and Northern England, General Manager for South Africa and U.K. Accounting Manager, the latter no doubt due to my previous accountancy training.

I turned them all down unseen, although the idea of a week's holiday in South Africa, while ostensibly checking out the job did have a certain appeal. However, Sarah's age and the civil unrest at that time in that apartheid ruled country ensured that I never gave the offer serious consideration.

My consistent refusals to move caused a certain amount of tut-tutting from my boss, the UK General Manager, Alec Lochhead, who was keen to point out that my attitude could lead me to becoming the forgotten man in the promotion stakes.

This should not have influenced me. I had my family, cricket and motorcycle racing needs being met and should have been satisfied. But my poetry had dried up and an air of discontent slowly grew.

One problem I never managed to resolve was our American masters' failure to understand how we could justify two offices within thirty miles of each other. It was difficult for them to accept that in those days Prestwick dealt only with transatlantic traffic, which was the bulk of our business, but all other cargo, including our domestic shipments for consolidation at Heathrow, had to be despatched via Glasgow's Abbotsinch airport.

This was no great problem when Emery's European head was a Scotsman, John Alexander, but when the European Head Office moved to Rotterdam under the stewardship of Jan Schenkels, the special status of Scotland was at an end.

Not that I had any problem with Jan, who was easily the best boss I had during my time as an Emery manager, it was just that the unique situation was lost on him.

I managed to hold that issue at arm's length during my tenure in Scotland, but on my departure the company made the sad mistake of closing the Glasgow office.

What made this such a painful decision was that, in addition to any commercial implications, the team at Abbotsinch were of the very highest quality. Eric, the export agent, Marion, the admin clerk and Peter, the driver always covered for each other, knew all their duties and never asked for help.

If I called into their office and found Peter typing air waybills, while Eric was out visiting a customer and Marion delivering a shipment, I learned not to ask questions. It would make sense.

It was some small comfort to me that I was able to help Eric, whose fiancee was Belgian, to get a job in our office in Brussels, where he proved a great success.

It was against this uncertain backdrop that I finally decided to make a move. Unfortunately, it was not a good choice.

Emery in the U.S.A. had recently introduced an aircraft chartering department, based in Elizabeth, New Jersey, and decided that an European counterpart was required in London.

Due to the several charters I had arranged from Prestwick to Australia and South America, mainly for several whisky manufacturers, I was seen as having the most experience in that branch of the business and was offered the job of setting up the London operation, with the goal of making it profitable within one year.

Since the only costs involved were my salary and travelling expenses, the corner of an office at Heathrow and the occasional help of one of our London service staff, it was not a particularly challenging target.

But it was with considerable sadness that I said goodbye to my old office, with its view, on a clear day, of the isle of Arran and to the staff who had been such a supportive and humorous group.

My first duty was to spend a couple of weeks over in New Jersey to see how the system operated. The U.S. Charter Manager, Joe Cannon, was a really charming guy who had years of experience under his belt. In addition to work, he also took me around some of the beauty spots on that lovely stretch of coastline, quite a contrast to the city of Elizabeth, parts of which looked like a car breakers yard.

However, it took me only one morning to discover that nothing of value could be learned from our U.S. end of the business, since chartering in the States was completely different to Europe. In the U.S. it was based on fixed tariff prices and finding the cargo space, whereas in Europe air chartering was all about coming up with the lowest price.

I filled out my time in New Jersey working as an extra clerk in the office, but with Joe's help did fulfil a long held ambition that had eluded me in Aberdeen, my first helicopter flights!

Back in London, it was a matter of making contacts and getting quotes - lots and lots of quotes.

My previous involvement in charters had been when the customer had approached me, but now the boot was on the other foot. I had simply no idea how many jobs it was necessary to quote for before one actually turned into an activity for which we got paid.

We achieved our target of profitability well within the one year timetable, but the hours of work that were ultimately wasted was quite demotivating and it left me regretting leaving my old home beyond Hadrian's wall.

Outside work, however, our personal circumstances had improved and the house we purchased in Foxcote, Wokingham remains my favourite of all the nine homes Ellen and I have shared since our marriage.

Our immediate vicinity was also very sociable, with Ellen and I being one of four couples who regularly dined and partied together.

Not for the first time, Ellen again reignited my cricketing career, again through a work colleague, and I found myself turning out for Wokingham, along stalwarts like Simon Goddard and the much admired Darwin Crawford, who I would team up with again years later with Berkshire Over 50s.

Back at work, my part-time assistant, Jon Jeffrey, was showing an aptitude for the work, but I was beginning to wonder if the rewards were worth the effort expended.

I had also heard from Joe Cannon that he felt Emery were cooling in their attitude to the ad hoc charter business, with the man with his name on the side of the trucks being more attracted to being the man with his name on the side of aircraft.

So, when out of the blue, Jan Schenkels invited Ellen and I out to dinner I had a feeling that my days in air charter were numbered. I took comfort from the fact that Ellen was invited, since I felt that he would not wish her to be witness to him sacking me, but I had not anticipated what he had in mind.

After the usual pleasantries had been exchanged and the menu thoroughly scrutinised, he asked, "How would you feel about joining my team in Rotterdam?"

Uncharted Territory

I had felt for some time that the end of my time in the Air Chartering Department, if not the department itself, was not too far in the future, but I certainly did not anticipate the offer that was now on the table.

It seems that our Head of Accounting in Europe had been indiscreet and had been dismissed. Actually "Accounting" is an exaggeration, since all our accounting was done in Scranton, Pennsylvania and the European Accounts offices were responsible only for paying our bills and invoicing and collecting monies due. This was not quite as simple as it sounds, for our people in Scranton had a well earned reputation for impatience, exacting standards and a very hard line on failure.

As such, this was not an attractive proposition for a real accountant, but my previous limited accounting experience, along with my ten years in the airfreight business, put me squarely in the frame.

Either way, the dinner must have gone well, for by the time it was over Jan had sold both Ellen and I on the move to Holland.

I don't know if Jan thought I may have second thoughts, but he wasted no time in announcing the move and the next thing I knew of the deal was a newspaper clipping from my hometown newspaper "The Tamworth Herald", which my mother sent to me.

"Rotterdam post for Dordon man", ran the headline.

Needless to say, the new job involved another training trip to the U.S.A., this time to both the Accounting Division in Scranton, Pennsylvania and the corporate Head Office in Wilton, Connecticut.
This would mean that all the names I had come to know and despise during my years in Birmingham and Prestwick would be made flesh and I would have the chance to see them as people and not merely unpleasant memos.

My trip had an inauspicious start. Due to some fuelling problem at Heathrow, my flight first had to call in at Paris. Then, when we finally got under way, it was announced that due to bad weather at New York we would be landing at a place called Windsor Locks. This was later rescinded and finally landed at JFK some ten hours after leaving London.

The terminal building was teeming with people whose flights had been delayed or cancelled and I had no confidence that my connecting flight to Scranton was going to get off the ground. I could not even find a check-in desk for it and was forced to join the queue of miserable, angry and desperate non-travellers at the besieged information desk

When I finally got to speak to a desk clerk, the very existence of my flight appeared to be in doubt and I was asked to stand aside, but only a few moments later a young man called out my name and asked me to follow him. I was surprised to find myself being hurried towards a fire exit and told not to move away.

There was nowhere to sit down but it was at least a quiet corner away from the hubbub of the rest of the building. Only half a dozen other people were standing around in that area, all looking as confused, tired and cheesed off as I felt.

However, only a few minutes later our guide reappeared, opened the fire exit and said, "Shall we go?"

We trooped outside behind him and glimpsed through the swirling snow the small aircraft to which he was leading us. We boarded and I was quite surprised to see my luggage stowed at the rear of the cabin. I took a seat at the front, where I could look into the cockpit area and over the pilots' shoulders to the wild night outside.

One of the few things I noticed as we taxied

out was that our small aircraft passed under the wing of a stationary Boeing 747.

We took off without incident and I learned that our flight was heading down through Pennsylvania and Ohio, stopping at three or four cities before terminating at Columbus.

I was the only passenger for Scranton, which was our first scheduled stop.

Nothing was visible outside my window except for the snow, whipping past horizontally, but I consoled myself with the thought that these pilots must fly this route every day and must be able to do the journey blindfold, which in effect, they were.

I found it quite disconcerting, therefore, when from my position of vantage behind the pilots, I heard one of them say, "Well, it's got to be down there somewhere!"

We landed at Scranton around midnight and it was with some envious looks from my fellow travellers that I wished them luck and disembarked.

I collected my luggage and entered the almost deserted arrivals hall. In fact the only other occupant was a stockily built man who I recognised from company newsletters. He stood up as I approached him and offered his hand.

"Hi, Alan," he said. "Welcome to Scranton. I'm Bob Wagner and you've made it in the nick of time. They've just announced that the airport is closed until further notice because of the snow."

Bob had been waiting there since nine p.m. and my flight was the last in or out of Scranton for three days.

I had arrived in Pennsylvania during one of the most severe spells of weather in the state's history, but if the climate was hostile, the welcome I received was anything but frosty.

It came as a pleasant surprise to discover that the authors of all the vitriolic memos were actually charming and gracious hosts, at least out of office hours. Their ability to switch off their work persona promptly on the stroke of five-thirty amazed me, even though they switched back on again at nine the following morning.

There were other peculiarities, such as only the men being allowed to smoke in the office. Similarly, only the men were allowed to wear trousers, in fact they were strongly encouraged to do so. Fortunately, I had gone prepared.

In addition, the working day was controlled by bells or buzzers, as I discovered on my first morning in the office.

I was being talked through some of the accounting procedures and reached down for my briefcase to take out my notebook. When I straightened up again, my tutor had disappeared. Looking around, I saw that the entire departmental staff had vanished. The only person in sight was the department head, Joan Ardizoni, who was looking out of her goldfish bowl office, clearly amused by my confusion. She came over to me and explained, "The buzzer went for their coffee break, but don't worry, the managers go at a different time."

Later in the day, I was walking down a corridor with the Vice-President Accounting, Ambrose Charnogursky, when a bell sounded and he pushed me unceremoniously into a doorway. Just in time, as a tidal wave of humanity swept past like crazed shoppers on the first day of the January sales.

"It's five-thirty," said Ambrose, "they rush out as fast as they can to queue for twenty minutes to get out of the car park."

He explained that his predecessor had been a martinet who was likely to fire anyone who looked up from their work when he entered the room. "I am trying to relax things a little", he added, "but it takes time. Old habits die hard."

Fortunately, as a visiting manager, I was spared most of Scranton's idiosyncrasies and was very well treated. In fact, they must have drawn up some kind of rota for looking after me, as I don't think I had dinner in my hotel once during my stay. I remember a College Basketball Match and a Guy Lombardo concert as two events on my social calendar.

I also learned, in those unguarded moments, that my predecessor had been held in contempt in Scranton because of his ready acquiescence to their many demands and realised that in order to get along with my new American colleagues I was going to have to give as good as I got.

My visit climaxed with a day trip to the corporate head office in Wilton, Connecticut, where I met, albeit briefly, the man with his name on the side of the trucks, who vaguely remembered seeing me somewhere before .

Going Dutch

While I was away, back in Wokingham, Ellen had again been left with most of the task of putting the house on the market and preparing for our move, a situation not eased by my being told of a two week visit to Europe by our internal auditors, who I would be expected to accompany.

A month into my new job, I had not yet seen my office and had to fly out to Frankfurt to meet up with the audit team.

As a former auditor myself, I was quite concerned over what kind of people I would be travelling with, since their visits are seldom anticipated with joy. Happily, I found their auditing style like my own, much more watchdog than bloodhound. Ed Kelly and Paul Gallagher were my new companions and I took an instant liking to them both.

Their work was thorough, but always open to humour, as I later found over the years with other company auditors, Pete La Scala and Rich Scott. The trip was perhaps a little trying for the accounting office managers we visited, since they were enduring both an audit and a first meeting with their new reporting senior.

The audit went well and I was able to turn my attention back to my family's relocation to

Holland and finally, after a major going-away party with our friends, we were on our way. When I say party, it was actually two parties, one in the afternoon for Sarah and her pals, followed by one for the grown-ups in the evening, but it actually merged into one long send-off which was memorably unrememberable.

So it was in fragile condition that we arrived next day at Rotterdam's Zestienhoven airport - Ellen, Sarah, Timmy the cat and I. It was only Timmy who received more than a casual glance from Customs and Immigration. A vet was summoned, Timmy pronounced fit and in answer to the Customs Officer's question as to the value of the cat, the vet burst out into peals of laughter. Thus embarrassed, Timmy was sentenced to six month's house arrest, with supervised toilet breaks.

We arrived at the apartment Jan had secured for us in Ommoord. 315 Cordell Hullplaats was a large, third floor flat with a bewildering number of doors leading off the main hallway. As the cupboard doors were the same as the room doors, I often found myself attempting to walk into a cupboard until I got used to the layout. As several of the rooms had more than one door, it was easy to find yourself somewhere you didn't intend to be.

Moving in was rather more complicated than

we expected, since it is the Dutch fashion when moving home to take everything moveable, including the lighting connections. As this meant that each room had two bare wires hanging from a hole in the ceiling, we had to go out and buy the items necessary to complete the electrical connections before we could even turn on a light.

Jan called in to welcome us to our new home and gamely stood on a chair to connect the wiring to the light in the living room. The whole fitting fell down ten minutes after he had left, but at least he had shown willing and gave us all a much needed laugh.

We also had to deal with our English cooker, which needed its wiring separated to plug into the standard wall sockets. This was a job for an electrician, but in our desperation I divided the wiring myself, crossed my fingers and to my surprise and delight, boiled some water for a cup of tea.

We had to notify the authorities to send an inspector to certify its safety, which they did after about two months. He gave it the thumbs up and said, "It is now O.K. for you to use the cooker".

I cannot imagine what he thought we had been doing in the meantime.

There was also the question of Sarah's

schooling and here Arie Montfrooy, Jan's deputy, came to our assistance in discussions with a Headmaster who could not, or would not, speak English.

We were told that Sarah would only be spoken to in Dutch, since this was the quickest way for her to learn. We thought this was rather harsh, but in fact she was chattering away to her school chums in a Rotterdam accent in a very short time. She also began to use her superior command of the language to take the lead in our shopping expeditions.

This did not stop her new pals from playing the occasional trick on the English kid, like letting her test the thickness of the ice on the canal to see if it was strong enough for skating.

Fortunately, this incident was witnessed by a kind lady, who brought a shivering Sarah home on the basket of her bicycle.

Her coat remained standing stiffly to attention long after Sarah had been bathed and put to bed.

By now I had finally been installed in my new office, a pleasant and spacious room on the third of a five floor commercial block in Alexanderpolder.

As Arie pointed out, "Your room faces west. You will be the first to notice the sea rushing in when the dykes burst. My office faces east - I'll be first to see the Russian tanks!"

Dutch humour.

On my first day, after Jan had introduced me to the rest of the staff, he took me aside and explained the anomaly of my position. I had inherited the problem of serving two masters, working for Jan for whom sales figures were the major concern, while answering to Accounting Division, to whom the protection of profit and reduction of costs were paramount. My simple task was to please both the people who liked spending money and those who liked saving it.

To Jan's credit, he did not sugar coat my dilemma.

As it turned out, I had some timely strokes of good fortune.

The various European managers already knew me as a line manager like themselves, with an understanding of their problems. I had already picked up from AD that their respect for my predecessor was not enhanced by his willing compliance to their every whim and I had also discovered during my audit trip that the accounts office managers in Europe were strangers to one another.

When these managers, almost entirely segregated from their own operating offices, started communicating and even meeting, they suddenly felt part of a team. When they also discovered that I intended to be their voice at AD instead of the head of AD's hammer, things rapidly improved.

We not only started exceeding the targets AD set for us, but setting and achieving higher targets of our own.

Rather that being beaten over the head with the Accounting Manual, we wrote our own, "International Accounting Manual", complete with pages headed "This page is intentionally blank", just like the original!

We sent copies to the Head Office and Accounting Division, where they were accepted without question and even, much to our amusement, quoted back to us!
Since all our accounting was in dollars, it had been AD's habit to rail against the European offices, when fixed items such as rents and hire contracts suddenly increased. Once we started to respond that we could not believe that they had failed to spot the changes in the exchange rates, they started to back off. They only understood dollars.

But the main benefit was that, by exceeding their targets, if not our own, they were off our backs and apart from those few occasions when things genuinely went awry Europe was spared the constant harassment of previous years.

I should mention that in company parlance "Europe" included the tiny offshore island of Africa!

Not that it was all fun, as the one distasteful part of my job was to investigate attempts at financial fraud in our offices.

Though there were only about seven or eight during my time in the job, they often took months to resolve and almost always ended in tears, with dismissals, one prison sentence and in the most tragic instance, an untimely death.

In all, I spent eight of my twenty years with the company in that job, based variously in Rotterdam, London and Zurich.

This period took me to and beyond the first forty years of my life that I intended to cover here, so at this point it would seem quite timely to say, "and we all lived happily ever after".

But that is only true in fairy tales and there were tragedies as well as triumphs to follow, some better told by others, some better not told at all.

While no one is about to tell how I inadvertently blew the cover of the CIA's man in a country in Central Africa, I'm sure Pete la Scala can tell all about the midnight flit from our hotel in Barcelona when we discovered that our investigation was itself being investigated.

Similarly, Ellen is best placed to recall her becoming a British Ladies Champion with her black powder muzzle loader and Sarah of her meeting with the playful Dalai Lama and her singing career with a blues band who even recorded some songs with my lyrics.

I'm sure Sarah's boys, Lugh and Finn will also have their tales to tell.

Postscript

It occurs to me that I have mentioned my poetry several times without having subjected you to any of it.

The example that follows may not be representative of my output, but it is a true story and qualifies to be part of my autobiography.

The incident it covers took place during the audit trip I made when I had just started working out of the Rotterdam Divisional Office but was still living in England.

Home for the Weekend

By moonlight, Lake Locarno was a fine, romantic sight
that lost its charm within an hour or two.
I thought upon the cruel fate that hounded me that night:
the awful journey I was living through.
When snow had started falling, earlier that day,
it gave no hint of what would come to pass.
By six Milan was choking as the snowstorm held its sway
and chaos reigned on roads that shone like glass.

221

I made it to the airport just around the time it closed.
Though offered food and lodging for the night,
I rather rashly opted for the other choice proposed
and would not weekend there without a fight.
The night-train bound for Paris had another coach attached
for some of us to take the extra space
and sometime after midnight we were finally despatched
with many hours of travel yet to face.

As we set off northward our progress seemed just fine.
The storm had eased and moonlit was the night.
But in the Alpine foothills drifting snow had blocked the line,
just as Lake Locarno came in sight.
As we waited for a snow plough to open up the tracks
our spirits ebbed again, without a doubt.
We thought no further troubles could be heaped upon our backs
when suddenly, the carriage lights went out.

Less immediately obvious, the heating, too, had failed
and soon the chill forced out all other thought.
As slowly on the windows icy tracings were detailed,

the shiv'ring passengers grew more distraught.
At last the cold was so severe that action was required.
Our luggage held a lot of extra clothes,
so we rummaged in the darkness until we were attired
with added insulation, head to toes.

When the snow-plough dug us out we continued into France,
where in the pre-dawn gloom the train stood still
in a tiny rural station, where stood an ambulance
to carry off the ones who'd suffered ill.
We were herded on the platform with gendarmes standing guard,
just like a group of wartime refugees.
With the faulty coach uncoupled, reloading was quite hard
as they pushed us in wherever we could squeeze.

Then a gendarme scrutinised me, though not a word was said.
I wondered why I'd earned his searching gaze.
Perhaps the underpants that I was wearing on my head
were not yet "de rigeur" in France those days.
The sun was shining brightly when in Paris we arrived,
too tired to care how many hours late.

In the station coffee bar, simply glad we had survived,
the coffee and the croissants tasted great.

I saw nothing of the city that passed above my head -
the Metro carried me to Charles de Gaulle.
Being back in my environment cleared away the dread
that I'd never, ever, make it home at all.
I slept my way to Heathrow and was home in time for tea,
looking forward to the chance to take my ease,
slightly tainted by the message my office left for me.
It read "Frankfurt, Monday morning, if you please!"

Alan Brown was born in March 1940 in the Warwickshire mining village of Dordon, where his parents ran the local cinema. After education at Queen Elizabeth 1st Grammar School in Atherstone, he studied accountancy with a Nuneaton practice before joining a Birmingham heavy machine tool manufacturer.

It was here that he met his future wife, Ellen, and accidentally stumbled into an unexpected career change. Asked to tend the company's Import Section until a full-time replacement was hired, he held that post for six years, leaving only when offered a job by one of the airfreight companies he used.

This was the start of twenty years with Emery Air Freight during which time he was based in Birmingham, Glasgow, London, Rotterdam and Zurich, travelling extensively through Europe, North America and South Africa,

His passion for cricket and poetry has remained with him since childhood and in addition to representing Berkshire in the Over 50s County Championship, he is a member of the Wokingham Library Poetry Group.

Alan and Ellen have been married now for over 50 years and their daughter, Sarah, whose education was spread across Scotland, Holland and England, is a partner in a therapy practice and with husband Alex has two sons, Lugh and Finn.